HMH SOCIAL STUDIES

**Interactive Reader and
Study Guide**

# United States
# Government
## Principles in Practice

# Contents

## How to Use this Book

The *Interactive Reader and Study Guide* was developed to help you get the most from your United States Government course. Using this book will help you master the content of the course while developing your reading and vocabulary skills. Reviewing the next few pages before getting started will make you aware of the many useful features in this book.

*Chapter Summary pages help you connect with the big picture. Studying them will keep you focused on the information you will need to be successful on your exams.*

**The Chapter Summary graphic organizers help you to summarize each chapter. They are a valuable study tool to help you prepare for important tests.**

**Answering each question will help you to understand the graphic organizer and ensure that you fully comprehend the content from the chapter.**

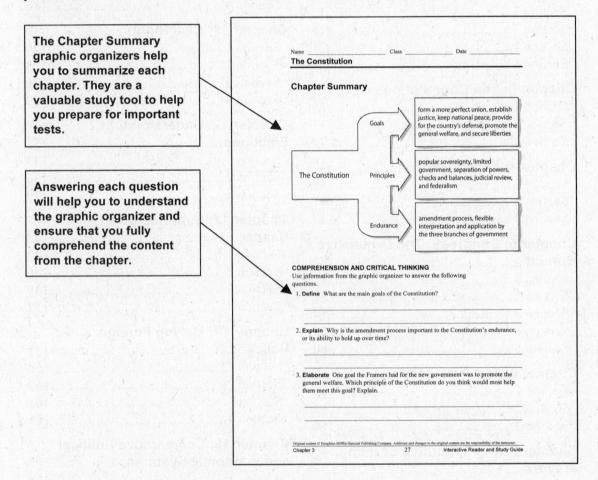

Name _____ Class _____ Date _____
**The Constitution**

**Chapter Summary**

The Constitution

Goals → form a more perfect union, establish justice, keep national peace, provide for the country's defense, promote the general welfare, and secure liberties

Principles → popular sovereignty, limited government, separation of powers, checks and balances, judicial review, and federalism

Endurance → amendment process, flexible interpretation and application by the three branches of government

**COMPREHENSION AND CRITICAL THINKING**
Use information from the graphic organizer to answer the following questions.

1. **Define** What are the main goals of the Constitution?

_____

2. **Explain** Why is the amendment process important to the Constitution's endurance, or its ability to hold up over time?

_____

3. **Elaborate** One goal the Framers had for the new government was to promote the general welfare. Which principle of the Constitution do you think would most help them meet this goal? Explain.

_____

Original content © Houghton Mifflin Harcourt Publishing Company. Additions and changes to the original content are the responsibility of the instructor.
Chapter 3                    27                    Interactive Reader and Study Guide

*Section Summary pages allow you to interact easily with the content and key terms from each section.*

**Clearly labeled page headers make navigating the book very simple.**

**The Main Idea statement from your textbook focuses your attention as you read the summaries.**

**The Key Terms and People from your textbook are provided with their definitions, making studying them easier.**

**The Taking Notes graphic organizers will help you to summarize the important points of each section.**

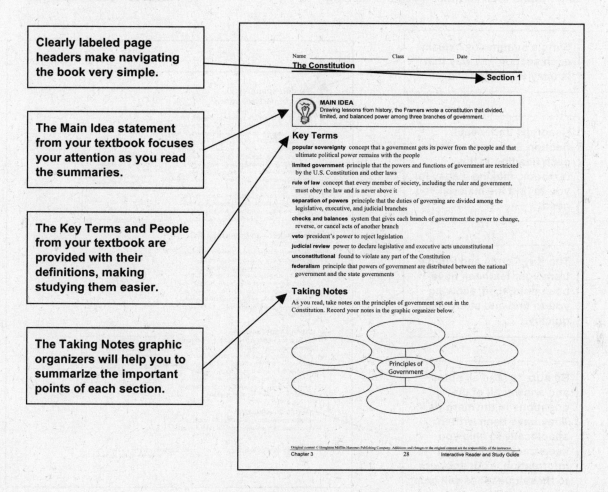

Name _____ Class _____ Date _____
**The Constitution**

                                                                    ▶ **Section 1**

**MAIN IDEA**
Drawing lessons from history, the Framers wrote a constitution that divided, limited, and balanced power among three branches of government.

**Key Terms**

**popular sovereignty** concept that a government gets its power from the people and that ultimate political power remains with the people

**limited government** principle that the powers and functions of government are restricted by the U.S. Constitution and other laws

**rule of law** concept that every member of society, including the ruler and government, must obey the law and is never above it

**separation of powers** principle that the duties of governing are divided among the legislative, executive, and judicial branches

**checks and balances** system that gives each branch of government the power to change, reverse, or cancel acts of another branch

**veto** president's power to reject legislation

**judicial review** power to declare legislative and executive acts unconstitutional

**unconstitutional** found to violate any part of the Constitution

**federalism** principle that powers of government are distributed between the national government and the state governments

**Taking Notes**

As you read, take notes on the principles of government set out in the Constitution. Record your notes in the graphic organizer below.

Principles of Government

Chapter 3                                28                    Interactive Reader and Study Guide

*Notes throughout the margins help you to interact with the content and understand the information you are reading.*

**Simple summaries explain each section in a way that is easy to understand.**

**Headings under each Section Summary relate to each heading in the textbook, making it easy for you to find the material you need.**

**The Key Terms and People from your textbook have been boldfaced, allowing you to find and study them quickly.**

**Be sure to read all notes and answer all of the questions in the margins. They have been written specifically to help you keep track of important information. Your answers to these questions will help you study for your tests.**

---

Name _____ Class _____ Date _____

Section 1 *continued*

## Section Summary

### GOALS OF THE CONSTITUTION

As they wrote the Constitution, the Framers had six definite goals for the new national government: form a more perfect union; establish justice, or laws; insure domestic tranquility, or national peace; provide for the common defense of the country; promote the general welfare of states and citizens; and secure the blessings of liberties won by fighting the American Revolution.

Although they knew what the government had to do, the Framers were at first uncertain of how to create the government itself. They knew from recent experience what could happen when a government suppressed the natural rights of its citizens. But the Framers also knew that citizens needed certain laws for the new nation to survive. A strong national government would be able to enforce these laws.

> What were the Framers afraid would happen if they designed a national government that was too powerful?
> _____
> _____

### PRINCIPLES OF GOVERNMENT IN THE CONSTITUTION

The Framers solved their dilemma over the balance of power by drawing upon six basic principles of governing: popular sovereignty, limited government, separation of powers, checks and balances, judicial review, and federalism. These principles ensure that the government's powers are subject to the will of the people and are presented in general terms throughout the Preamble, seven Articles, and 27 Amendments of the Constitution.

### POPULAR SOVEREIGNTY

**Popular sovereignty** is the idea that a government gets it powers from the people it governs. The Framers began the Constitution with this idea: "We the People of the United States…do ordain and establish this Constitution…" Today, people participate in popular sovereignty in every election, when they choose and vote for the citizens they wish to lead their community, state, or country.

> How is voting a good example of popular sovereignty?
> _____
> _____

### LIMITED GOVERNMENT

**Limited government** is the idea that the powers of government are restricted by the U.S. Constitution and

Chapter 3          29          Interactive Reader and Study Guide

---

Name _____ Class _____ Date _____

# Foundations of Government

## Chapter Summary

| | |
|---|---|
| Around the world, governments have different purposes. These purposes vary according to the theory on which a government is based and how power is organized. | American democracy is built around the ideals of liberty, equality, and self-government, as well as a free-enterprise economic system. |

## COMPREHENSION AND CRITICAL THINKING
Use information from the graphic organizer to answer the following questions.

1. **Identify** What ideals characterize the U.S. government?

   _____

   _____

2. **Compare** Why do the purposes of governments differ?

   _____

   _____

3. **Develop** Judging from the core ideals of American democracy, what do you think are some of purposes of the U.S. government?

   _____

   _____

## Foundations of Government

**MAIN IDEA**
Understanding major political ideas and classic forms of government will help you understand the purpose of government.

# Key Terms

**government** the formal structures and institutions through which decisions are made for a body of people

**power** the government's authority and ability to get things done

**policy** any decision made by government in pursuit of a particular goal

**state** a political community made up by a group of people that lives within a clearly defined territory

**sovereignty** the supreme power of the state to act within its territory

**politics** the process by which government makes and carries out decisions as to whose interests will be served in society

**legitimacy** when rulers are seen as right and proper by important segments of a nation's population

**divine right of kings** a theory put forth by Jacques-Bénigne Bossuet that the king is answerable only to God, not the people he ruled

**social contract theory** theory of rule that says the first governments formed as a result of people agreeing among themselves to submit to the authority of a state, which in turn would protect and support them

# Taking Notes

As you read, take notes on the purposes of government. Record your notes in a graphic organizer like this one.

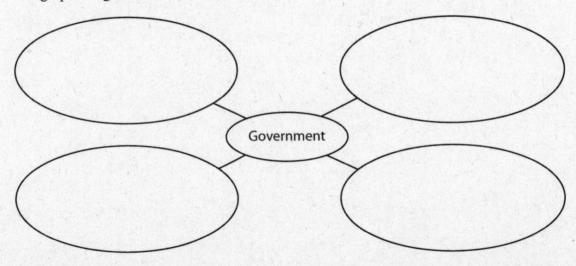

# Section Summary

## WHAT IS GOVERNMENT?

**Government** is the formal structures and institutions through which decisions are made for a body of people. A government is a typically composed of three things: people, powers, and policies. The people of government include everyone from elected officials to public servants who carry out local, state, and national government business. A government's **power** is its authority and ability to get things done. In American government, this includes legislative, executive, and judicial powers. The **policies** of a government are any decisions it makes in pursuit of a goal, ranging from specific laws to general programs or actions.

## CHARACTERISTICS OF A STATE

Most modern governments are run within a **state**, a political community made up by a group of people that lives within a clearly defined territory. A state is typically defined by four characteristics. First, a state is made up of territory, land whose formal borders are recognized by other states. Second, a state has a population. Third, a state has a government, recognized by its people, which creates and enforces laws. Finally, a state has **sovereignty**, or the supreme power to act within its own territory. Although this power does mean the government is the highest authority in the state, the government remains subject to the same laws as its people.

> Give an example of a government decision that classifies as a policy.
>
> _____
>
> _____
>
> _____

## FUNCTIONS OF GOVERNMENT

Today, the majority of governments share five important functions. First, a government must ensure national security, often by both funding defense forces and by fostering international diplomacy.

Second, a government must maintain order. This function consists of establishing laws in order to protect people and property. The government is responsible both for enforcing these laws and for punishing those persons who refuse to follow them.

Third, a government needs to resolve conflict. It does this through **politics**, the process by which government makes and carries out decisions as to

> The government is responsible for creating laws. What else is it expected to do with these laws?
>
> _____
>
> _____

whose interests will be served in society. These decisions are made by officials elected by the state's people, many of whose wants and needs are very different. The government must therefore make compromises within the political process before creating new laws and enacting new programs.

Fourth, a government must provide the services its citizens need. These services are paid for with taxes, which are used to build roads, fund education, provide public housing, and much more.

Finally, the government must provide for the public good, or the needs and interests of the people as a whole. One example of government fulfilling this purpose is regulating food safety, an action that protects all Americans. As American society and culture has changed over the centuries, citizens and government have needed to reevaluate what defines "public good" and even "public."

> **Name another way the government provides for the public good.**
>
> _____
>
> _____
>
> _____

## THEORIES OF RULE

There are various political philosophies as to why people allow governments to rule them. At the heart of these philosophies is the notion of **legitimacy**, the idea that rulers are seen as right and proper by important segments of a nation's population. People, therefore, will voluntarily accept governance.

In the past, European kings attempted to claim their legitimacy was a result of the **divine right of kings**, declaring that they received the right to rule from God directly. Yet many philosophers who came both before and after these claims did not agree. As far back as ancient Greece, philosophers wrote of natural law, a system of rules derived from the natural world that includes the idea that individuals possess natural rights. In the 1600s, **social contract theory**, which states that the first governments formed as a result of people agreeing among themselves to submit to the authority of the state, surfaced. Philosophers Thomas Hobbes, John Locke, and Jean-Jacques Rousseau built upon this theory, proposing ideas of government that depended on cooperation among citizens, consent of the governed in exchange for protection of natural rights, and a combination of a social contract and responsiveness to the "general will" of citizens.

> **Under the social contract theory, how were the first governments created?**
>
> _____
>
> _____
>
> _____

## Foundations of Government

**MAIN IDEA**
Different forms of government are categorized based on who exercises authority and how power is organized.

# Key Terms

**monarchy** a system of government headed by one person, such as a king or queen, who exercises absolute authority

**dictatorship** a system of rule in which one person, a dictator, or a small group of people can hold unlimited power over government

**oligarchy** a dictatorship led by a small group of people; means "rule by a few"

**direct democracy** a system of government in which citizens meet regularly in a popular assembly to discuss issues and vote for leaders

**republic** an indirect form of democracy that places political decision making at least one step away from the people; instead, people elect representatives to make decisions on their behalf

**unitary system** a system of government in which sovereignty, or ultimate authority, rests in a single national government

**federal system** a system of government in which power over people and territory is divided between a national government and smaller, regional levels of government

**confederal system** a system of government in which a confederation of independent states form a central government to pursue common interests

**presidential system** a system of government distinguished by having a president who is elected by the people for a limited term of office

**parliamentary system** a system of government in which the legislative and executive branches are combined

# Taking Notes

As you read, takes notes on different types of government systems. Record your notes in a chart like this one.

| Form | Details |
|------|---------|
|      |         |
|      |         |
|      |         |
|      |         |

# Section Summary

## THE CLASSIC FORMS

The most common form of government in world history has been the **monarchy**, a system of government headed by one person who inherits power, such as a king or queen. In an absolute monarchy, the monarch's power is unlimited, but in the more common constitutional monarchy, the monarch is a ceremonial figure, less powerful than other parts of the government.

In a **dictatorship**, one person—called a dictator—or a group of people—called an **oligarchy**—hold unlimited power over government. The strength of dictators, who have usually taken over the former government by force, varies. Some are independent of religion; others, called theocracies, are linked closely to religion. The most powerful are totalitarian governments, which attempt to dominate all aspects of society, including religion and the economy.

Democracy, literally meaning "rule by the people," is a much different form of government. In a **direct democracy**, citizens meet regularly to discuss and address issues and vote directly for leaders. Since this system is hard to accomplish in large nations, many countries, including the United States, choose to be **republics** (sometimes called representative democracies). In a republic, the people elect representatives to make decisions for them.

> Is a monarch more powerful in a constitutional monarchy or an absolute monarchy?
> _____
> _____

> What is the difference between a direct democracy and a republic?
> _____
> _____
> _____

## ORGANIZING NATIONAL POWER

There are a variety of ways in which countries govern their smaller administrative units, such as states, cities, and provinces. Most countries employ the **unitary system**, through which ultimate authority, or sovereignty, rests in a single national government. While local governments can still exist in the unitary system, the national government can overrule their decisions and even abolish them completely.

In a **federal system**, invented by the Framers of the U.S. Constitution, power over people and land is divided between the national government and regional levels of government, such as state governments. Unlike a unitary system, in a federal system neither level of government can abolish the other nor can each operate completely independently of the other.

The third organizational form of national power, the **confederal system**, is uncommon today. Under this system, independent states govern their own people and land while still maintaining a weak central government. This central government is only responsible for functions important to the group of states, or confederation, such as defense and trade.

> What is the difference between regional levels of government in a federal system and those in a confederal system?
>
> _____
>
> _____
>
> _____

## PRESIDENTS AND PARLIAMENTS

Democracies, though they can vary somewhat in structure, follow either a presidential political system or a parliamentary political system. The United States' government is an example of a **presidential system**. In this system, besides acting as the head of state, the president is also the head of the executive branch. His or her duties as chief executive range from setting foreign policy to appointing cabinet members to introducing legislation.

Since the U.S. government structure includes separation of powers, the president's authority is balanced by the way the legislature can check his or her actions. The president and Congress must work together to make sure the daily business of government gets done. Unfortunately, this system of divided government can sometimes result in political gridlock; when the president and Congress disagree, the political process can come to a halt.

Gridlock is less of a problem in **parliamentary systems** since the executive and legislative branches are one entity. Members of the legislature, called parliament, are elected by the people. These officials in turn choose the prime minister, who is both the head of state and the leader of the majority party in parliament. If the prime minister loses support of his or her party, he or she must resign, at which points parliament chooses another head of state.

> Why is gridlock less of a problem in parliamentary systems?
>
> _____
>
> _____
>
> _____

Critics of the parliamentary system feel that it is wrong that the voting public cannot directly elect a prime minister and that the prime minister is too much under the control of parliament. But supporters believe that it is easier to pass laws in this kind of united system than in the presidential system.

## Foundations of Government

 **MAIN IDEA**
American democracy is characterized by core democratic ideals and principles,
as well as by the free enterprise system.

# Key Terms

**ideal** a conception of something in its most perfect form

**liberty** the ability of people to act and think as they choose, as long as their choices do no
harm to the liberty or well-being of others

**equality** the principle that all people possess a fundamental, moral worth that entitles
them to fair treatment under the law and equal opportunity in all aspects of life

**self-government** the belief that ordinary people could aspire to rule themselves and do
so as political equals

**majority rule** a decision-making system in which the candidate who receives more than
half the votes cast, or more votes than any other candidate, wins the election

**minority rights** the political rights held by groups who make up less than half of the
population

**liberal democracy** a form of democracy that protects the rights of the minority

**free enterprise** an economic system in which people and businesses make their own
choices about how best to produce, distribute, and exchange goods and services, with
limited interference from the government

# Taking Notes

As you read, take notes on democracy in the United States. Record your
notes in a graphic organizer like this one.

# Section Summary

## IDEALS OF AMERICAN DEMOCRACY

American democracy is centered around three **ideals**, or conceptions of something in its most perfect form: liberty, equality, and self-government. Over the centuries, these ideals have been applied to more and more of the American population—an excellent example of how American democracy is constantly evolving.

**Liberty**, also called freedom, is the ability of people to think and act as they choose, so long as their choices do not harm the liberty or well-being of other people. The Framers designed the Constitution and the Bill of Rights to specifically protect this ideal. For example, Americans' basic rights are protected from government interference by the First Amendment, which protects free speech, assembly, the press, and religion. The Framers also ensured that Americans would be able to exercise these protected rights, such as exercising their right to counsel or to vote.

**Equality**, the second ideal, is the principle that all people possess a fundamental, moral worth that entitles them to fair treatment under the law and equal opportunity. Yet some groups of Americans, including Native Americans and enslaved African Americans, were not always treated with equality. The American people and their government have had to make changes to guarantee that equality in its fullest form does indeed exist and is adequately balanced with the ideal of liberty.

**Self-government** is the third ideal at the heart of American democracy. This ideal is the belief that ordinary people can aspire to rule themselves and can do so as political equals. The Declaration of Independence proclaimed the importance of self-government to the American colonists, and the American Revolution was fought to make self-government possible. Under self-government, the power of the government lies primarily with the people, who have the right to keep or abolish the government as they see fit.

> **How is Americans' freedom of speech an example of liberty?**
> _____
> _____

> **Explain equality in your own words.**
> _____
> _____
> _____
> _____

## PRINCIPLES OF AMERICAN DEMOCRACY

Five key principles underlie the success and continuity of American democracy. First, the worth of the individual is held in high esteem. If a person is allowed to pursue his or her own individual freedoms and ambitions, the Framers believed, he or she is more likely to reach their highest potential.

Second, American democracy depends on the rule of law. According to this principle, no government official is above the law.

Third, both **majority rule**, the idea that the candidate with more than half of votes cast or more votes than any other candidate wins, and **minority rights**, the political rights of those who make up less than half of the population, are respected. This mutual protection of rights is an example of how American democracy is also a **liberal democracy**, a form of democracy that protects the rights of the minority.

Fourth, compromise is key to the success of democracy. Faced with the diverse needs and wants of Americans, opposing groups in government must compromise in order to continue the political process.

Finally, American democracy depends on the participation of citizens. People must educate themselves on issues in order to vote wisely, hold their leaders accountable, protest what they consider wrongful government actions, and generally be as involved as possible in the political process.

> Why is liberal democracy necessary to American democracy?
> _____
> _____
> _____

## FREE ENTERPRISE

Economic freedom is the basis of the American **free enterprise** system, which allows people and businesses to make their own economic choices about how best to produce, distribute, and exchange goods and services. Furthermore, free enterprise protects the products and services a person produces and his or her other private property.

In this kind of free market, the government is largely uninvolved. The theory behind this design is that with little government interference, people and businesses will compete to offer better products at lower prices. As the American economy has evolved, some government intervention has become necessary; however, the national economy remains mainly open.

> Why is it important that government plays only a minor role in a free market?
> _____
> _____
> _____

## Origins of American Government

# Chapter Summary

## COMPREHENSION AND CRITICAL THINKING
Use information from the graphic organizer to answer the following questions.

1. **Describe**  What prompted colonists to rebel in the mid-1700s?

_____

_____

2. **Analyze**  Were you surprised to learn that the Constitution was heavily debated before it was ratified? Explain.

_____

_____

3. **Elaborate**  After the country's experience with the Articles of Confederation, why do you think the compromises made at the Constitutional Convention were so important?

_____

_____

_____

# Origins of American Government

 **MAIN IDEA**
American democracy was shaped by our English political heritage, colonial experiments in self-government, as well as a range of intellectual influences.

## Key Terms

**bicameral** two-chamber

**Magna Carta** an English document signed by King John in 1215 that instituted that "rule of law" and protected certain individual rights

**Petition of Right** an English document signed by King Charles in 1628 that required monarchs to obtain Parliament's approval before levying new taxes and said that monarchs could not unlawfully imprison people, force citizens to house soldiers, or establish military rule during times of peace

**English Bill of Rights** an English document passed by Parliament in 1689 that limited monarchs' power to enact laws, raise taxes, or keep an army without Parliament's consent; guaranteed Parliament the privilege of free speech; and gave all people protection from cruel and unusual punishment

**Fundamental Orders of Connecticut** a 1639 set of laws that limited the power of the government and gave all free men the right to choose the people to serve as judges

**proprietary colony** a colony based on a grant of land by the English monarch to a proprietor

**royal colonies** colonies directly controlled by the king through an appointed governor

**charter colonies** colonies operated under charters agreed to by the colony and the king

## Taking Notes

As you read, take notes on the political ideas and historical events that shaped government in the English colonies. Record your notes in the graphic organizer below.

| Ideas | Events |
|---|---|
|  |  |
|  |  |
|  |  |
|  |  |

# Section Summary

## ENGLISH POLITICAL HERITAGE

When the first English settlers arrived in North America, they brought their political heritage with them, ready to adjust it as necessary for their new home. This heritage included the idea of representative government, which in England had evolved from a king's advisory council to a **bicameral**, or two-house, legislature called Parliament. This legislature was made up of the noble-dominated House of Lords and the less prestigious House of Commons who worked to limit the power of English monarchs. One of the first efforts toward limited government was **Magna Carta**. This English document signed by King John in 1215 instituted the "rule of law" and eventually protected the individual rights of most citizens.

England's focus on protecting individual rights further developed with the creation of the 1628 **Petition of Right**. This document, which was signed by King Charles, required monarchs to obtain Parliament's approval before levying new taxes and banned monarchs from unlawfully imprisoning people, forcing citizens to house soldiers, or establishing military rule during times of peace. In the years that followed, Parliament's power grew and the monarchy's authority weakened, circumstances that eventually led to a constitutional monarchy. The **English Bill of Rights** greatly contributed to this, forbidding monarchs to enact laws, raise taxes, or keep an army without Parliament's consent; guaranteeing Parliament the privilege of free speech; and giving all people protection from cruel and unusual punishment.

> What ideas of government did settlers bring with them from England?
>
> _____
> _____
> _____
> _____

## THE ENGLISH COLONIES

As they settled the colonies, the English settlers drew on their political heritage to establish societies and laws. The Jamestown House of Burgesses, established in 1619, was an experiment in representative democracy, and the Mayflower Compact was an agreement to govern according to majority rule and the consent of the people. In 1639 the **Fundamental Orders of Connecticut**, a set of laws that limited the power of the government and gave all free men the right to choose the people to serve as judges, was approved by Connecticut colonists. Laws adopted within the Massachusetts Bay Colony also protected several individual rights.

However, all of these laws and practices were created within colonies that existed under charters, or agreements by which the English king gave settlers the right to establish a colony and promised them "the rights of Englishmen." There were three types of colonies. A **proprietary colony** was based on a grant of land by the English monarch to a proprietor, who could appoint all officials and make all laws. A **royal colony** was directly controlled by the king through an appointed governor. Royal colonies had two-house legislatures, in which members of the lower house were elected but members of the upper house were appointed by the king. Finally, a **charter colony** operated under charters agreed to by the colony and the king and therefore had the most independence. Colonists elected a legislature that made laws and appointed a governor. By the time the American Revolution began, there were only two charter colonies, and the king's attempts to control royal colonies—which most other colonies were at that time—greatly angered colonists.

| How did royal colonies differ from charter colonies? |
| --- |
| _____ |
| _____ |
| _____ |
| _____ |

## INTELLECTUAL INFLUENCES

The developing American democracy also drew on intellectual influences outside of Great Britain. The Framers of the U.S. Constitution would turn to ancient Greek and Roman scholars, Renaissance scholar Niccolò Machiavelli, and French philosopher Charles de Montesquieu for ideas about republicanism, or representative government, and the role the people should play within a republic. The Framers would also incorporate Judeo-Christian beliefs in human equality and the divine origin of rights into their design for a new American government. Finally, the Framers reviewed the thoughts of Enlightenment thinkers like John Locke and Jean-Jacques Rousseau in order to best understand ideas such as natural rights and economic and civil liberties.

| What ideas did the Framers borrow from Enlightenment thinkers? |
| --- |
| _____ |
| _____ |
| _____ |
| _____ |

# Origins of American Government

**MAIN IDEA**
The British imposed new policies on the American colonies, sparking rebellion, and in time, the American Revolution.

## Key Terms

**New England Confederation** confederation formed between the Plymouth, Connecticut, Massachusetts Bay, and New Haven colonies to defend against Native Americans and nearby Dutch colonies

**Iroquois Confederation** a powerful alliance of six Native American nations—the Mohawk, Oneida, Onondaga, Cayuga, Seneca, and Tuscarora

**Albany Plan of Union** a plan proposed by Benjamin Franklin that called for a council of representatives appointed by the colonial assemblies and a president general appointed by the king

**Stamp Act** Parliament's first attempt to tax American colonists directly, which required a government tax stamp on paper goods and all legal documents

**First Continental Congress** first general meeting of the colonies in Philadelphia, Pennsylvania, called by the Virginia and Massachusetts assemblies at which delegates sent King George III the Declaration of Resolves

**Second Continental Congress** second general meeting of the colonies in Philadelphia, Pennsylvania, at which delegates took strong measures against the Crown

**Virginia Declaration of Rights** declaration issued by the Virginia House of Burgesses that proclaimed "all men are by nature equally free and independent and have certain inherent rights" and that likely inspired parts of the Declaration of Independence

## Taking Notes

As you read, take notes on the causes and effects of the American Revolution. Record your notes in the graphic organizer below.

| Causes | | Effects |
|---|---|---|
| 1.<br><br>2.<br><br>3. | The American Revolution | 1.<br><br>2.<br><br>3. |

# Section Summary

## THE ROAD TO INDEPENDENCE

The American colonies first took steps toward unity in 1643, with the creation of the **New England Confederation**, formed between the Plymouth, Connecticut, Massachusetts Bay, and New Haven colonies to defend themselves against Native Americans and nearby Dutch colonies. Later, in 1754 and during the French and Indian War, the British government asked the colonies to sign a treaty with the **Iroquois Confederation**, a powerful alliance of six Native American nations—the Mohawk, Oneida, Onondaga, Cayuga, Seneca, and Tuscarora—whose support would help the British defeat the French. Not long after, Benjamin Franklin, inspired by what he had learned about Iroquois government, proposed the **Albany Plan of Union**, which called for a council of representatives appointed by the colonial assemblies and a president general appointed by the king. While both the colonial assemblies and the British government rejected Franklin's proposal, it would eventually inspire the U.S. Constitution.

By the mid-1700s, there were more reasons for colonial unifications. Beginning with 1764's Sugar Act, Great Britain began imposing new trade restrictions and taxes on the colonists. The colonists had no representation in Parliament and felt that taxes imposed by anyone outside of colonial assemblies were unfair, especially after the passage of the 1765 **Stamp Act**, Parliament's first attempt to tax American colonists directly that required a government tax stamp on paper goods and all legal documents. The Act was repealed after much protest, but new taxes were soon imposed in its place. Colonial resistance and confrontations with British troops—including the deadly 1770 Boston Massacre—increased, and communication among the colonies grew as colonists shared information in letters. After the Boston Tea Party in 1773, the king and Parliament punished the colonies with what were soon called the Intolerable Acts, a set of harsh laws that included an end to self-rule in Massachusetts and the quartering of British troops in private homes.

> **What was the purpose of the New England Confederation?**
>
> _____
>
> _____
>
> _____

> **Why did the American colonists feel that the new taxes were unfair?**
>
> _____
>
> _____
>
> _____
>
> _____

## THE CONTINENTAL CONGRESSES

Despite the Intolerable Acts, most colonists hoped a compromise could be reached that would lead to a removal of the taxes. To this end, the **First Continental Congress**, the first general meeting of the colonies in Philadelphia, Pennsylvania, met in fall of 1774. Delegates issued a Declaration of Resolves, which included a call for a repeal of the Intolerable Acts. After their demands were rejected, the colonies met in the **Second Continental Congress**, a second general meeting where delegates organized the Continental Army. Once a last petition to the king was rejected, the Congress organized as a government and prepared for war—and independence. Thomas Paine's bestselling political pamphlet *Common Sense* supported the Congress's decisions, declaring that independence was now a "common sense" action and inspiring hundreds of thousands of colonists.

> **What did the Second Continental Congress prepare for once the king rejected their last petition?**
>
> _____
>
> _____
>
> _____

## THE DECLARATION OF INDEPENDENCE

On July 2, 1776, delegates at the Continental Congress passed a resolution to declare independence from Great Britain. Virginia delegate Thomas Jefferson wrote most of the resolution's formal statement within a two-week period in June, probably drawing heavily on the **Virginia Declaration of Rights**, a declaration issued by the Virginia House of Burgesses that proclaimed "all men are by nature equally free and independent and have certain inherent rights." The resulting Declaration of Independence, adopted on July 4, reflected the philosophy of John Locke, discussing people's "unalienable" natural rights and the need for the "consent of the governed." A new nation had been formed.

## THE STATE CONSTITUTIONS

By 1780 all 13 colonies had adopted written constitutions, which included ideas about republicanism that would soon influence the U.S. Constitution. While voting rights varied, all of the constitutions established legislatures of elected representatives, as well as judicial and executive branches, and limited the powers of the legislative and executive branches. Many also included bills of rights.

> **What did the state constitutions have in common?**
>
> _____
>
> _____

# Origins of American Government

 **MAIN IDEA**
The states' first attempts to build a national government, the Articles of Confederation, proved too weak to last.

## Key Terms

**Articles of Confederation** the first constitution of the United States

**ratify** formally approve

**Northwest Ordinance** 1787 legislation that established a plan for settling the Northwest Territory

**Shays's Rebellion** a rebellion of Massachusetts farmers who were angry at the prospect of losing their land

## Taking Notes

As you read, take notes on the advantages and disadvantages of the Articles of Confederation. Record your notes in the graphic organizer below.

| The Articles of Confederation | |
|---|---|
| Advantages | Disadvantages |
| | |

# Section Summary

## FIRST NATIONAL GOVERNMENT

In anticipation of declaring independence, the Second
Continental Congress began designing a plan for a
national government in June 1776. By June 12, 1777,
the Congress adopted the first constitution of the
United States, the **Articles of Confederation**, a name
reflective of the friendly confederation the delegates
wished the former colonies to become.

However, not all of the states were ready to **ratify**,
or formally approve, the Articles. In particular, small
states were afraid that large states with claims to
western lands would become too powerful. Once the
Congress agreed that the entire Confederation would
control the Western lands, ratification was completed
in 1781.

The Articles left most power to the states, creating
only a weak federal government with no executive or
judicial branches. While a one-house legislature called
Congress was created—in which each state had one
vote—at least nine states would have to approve
legislation in order to pass it, and the approval of all
13 was needed to approve any changes to the Articles
themselves. Congress was given the power to act on
matters of common interest to the states, admit new
states and organize western lands, organize a postal
service, coin and borrow money, appoint military
officers and raise an army, declare war, make peace,
and conduct foreign policy. The states retained all
other powers, including those to collect taxes, enforce
national laws, and contribute funds to the national
government as they deemed necessary.

> How would legislation pass
> in the new Congress,
> according to the Articles of
> Confederation?
>
> _____
>
> _____
>
> _____

## WEAKNESSES OF THE ARTICLES

There were many problems with the Articles of
Confederation, including the lack of a federal
executive branch to carry out laws and a federal court
system to apply them. Also, since the Articles did not
allow Congress to tax the states, it had no formal way
of raising money—and the states chose not to
contribute much. Furthermore, Congress could not
regulate commerce between states, even when
interstate tax laws were unfair, and its power to coin
money conflicted with the states' same power,

> Did the new national
> government successfully
> raise money? Explain.
>
> _____
>
> _____

resulting in several different currencies in circulation. Finally, very rarely did 9 of the 13 states agree to pass legislation, making it difficult for Congress to act decisively.

## PRESSURES FOR STRONGER GOVERNMENT

It gradually became obvious to Americans and their new government that the Articles of Confederation would not work as a constitution. While in 1787 Congress did manage to pass the **Northwest Ordinance**—legislation that established a plan for settling the Northwest Territory, banned slavery in the territory, created a system for admitting new states, and guaranteed certain rights to settlers—it met little success in other areas, especially when it came to raising money to pay national war debts. Events such as **Shays's Rebellion**, a rebellion by thousands of Massachusetts farmers angry at the prospect of losing their land, highlighted Congress's military and economic weaknesses.

In March 1785, George Washington and representatives from Virginia and Maryland met at Washington's Mount Vernon home to discuss how to resolve a trade dispute between the states. When the talks were successful, certain state officials were inspired to ask Congress to call a meeting of all the states to revise the Articles of Confederation. The meeting was scheduled for May, 1787 in Philadelphia.

> **What happened in Massachusetts that further highlighted Congress's weaknesses?**
>
> _____
>
> _____

## Origins of American Government

**MAIN IDEA**
Delegates at the Constitutional Convention compromised on key issues to create a plan for a strong national government.

## Key Terms

**Framers**  the delegates to the Constitutional Convention

**Virginia Plan**  a proposed plan for government that called for a strong central government divided into three branches—legislative, executive, and judicial—each with the power to check the others; included a bicameral legislature in which membership would be based on a state's population

**New Jersey Plan**  another proposed plan for government that called for a strong central government divided into three branches; included a unicameral legislature in which each state would get one vote

**Great Compromise**  plan of government that combined elements of the Virginia and New Jersey plans; included a bicameral legislature in which membership in one house would be based on state population and membership in the other would be limited to two members per state

**Three-Fifths Compromise**  the resolution to a dispute over how enslaved people should be counted within a population; provided that three-fifths of the enslaved people in a state would be counted when determining a state's population

## Taking Notes

As you read, take notes on the writing of the U.S. Constitution. Record your notes in the graphic organizer below.

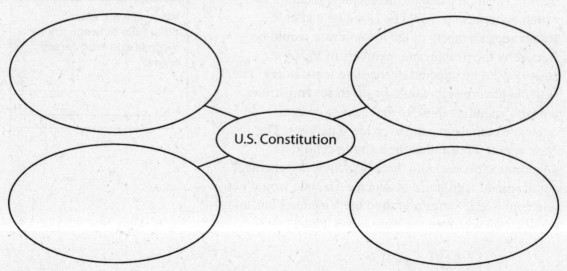

U.S. Constitution

# Section Summary

## DRAFTING A NEW CONSTITUTION

On May 25, 1787, 12 of the 13 states—Rhode Island chose not to participate—met in Philadelphia to revise the Articles of Confederation—a task that would soon change to designing an entirely new government. Delegates kept all meeting proceedings confidential. Each state received one vote and only a simple majority was required for any decisions. Almost all of the attendees had some form of government experience, and many had served in the Continental Army. George Washington served as president of the convention. James Madison—now known as Father of the Constitution—played a key role in planning the convention and calling for a new government. Today, all delegates at the convention are called **Framers** of the Constitution.

> Did large states have more voting power than small states at the convention? Explain.
>
> _____
>
> _____
>
> _____

## RIVAL PLANS

Only days into the convention, it became clear to delegates that the Articles of Confederation would need to be replaced with a plan for a stronger government. Two plans were proposed shortly thereafter.

The **Virginia Plan** called for a strong central government divided into three branches—legislative, executive, and judicial—each with the power to check the others, and included a bicameral legislature in which membership would be based on a state's population. Members of the lower house would be elected by the people, and members of the upper house would be selected by the state legislatures. The national government would be given several strong powers, including those to make laws, control interstate commerce, and override state laws. The **New Jersey Plan** called for a strong central government divided into three branches, and included a unicameral legislature in which each state would get one vote. Large states preferred the Virginia Plan, and small states preferred the New Jersey Plan.

> What was the main difference between the Virginia and New Jersey plans?
>
> _____
>
> _____

## CONFLICT AND COMPROMISE

After a long period of deadlock, delegates finally agreed to an alternate plan on July 16, 1787. The **Great Compromise**, as it became known, combined elements of the Virginia and New Jersey plans. It included a bicameral legislature in which membership in the lower house, the House of Representatives, would be based on state population and membership in the upper house, the Senate, would be limited to two members per state. House members would be elected by the people and Senate members would be selected by the state legislatures.

With a decision on the design of government finalized, delegates next needed to compromise on issues surrounding slavery. The first issue involved how enslaved people should be counted as part of a state's population. The **Three-Fifths Compromise** eventually settled this dispute between northern and southern delegates by providing that three-fifths of the enslaved people in a state would be counted when determining a state's population. Delegates also reached a compromise on the future importation of slaves, which the northern delegates resisted but southern delegates supported. It was agreed that the Atlantic slave trade would be protected from interference by Congress until 1808—in exchange for the agreement that only a simple majority would be needed in each house of Congress to regulate commerce.

Delegates also compromised on how the president should be elected. The president would be chosen by state electors—who themselves could be elected by the people—unless no one candidate received a majority of votes, in which case the House of Representatives would choose the president.

By September 1787, a constitution reflecting the delegates' decisions and compromises was complete. Thirty-nine delegates from 12 states signed the document—three delegates abstained because of the absence of a Bill of Rights—and the convention adjourned on September 17. The American people would now need to ratify the new U.S. Constitution.

> **How were enslaved people counted as part of the population under the Three-Fifths Compromise?**
> _____
> _____
> _____

> **Why did a few delegates choose not to sign the Constitution?**
> _____
> _____
> _____

# Origins of American Government

**MAIN IDEA**
Before the Constitution could take effect, a heated debate between those in favor of the Constitution and those who opposed it took place in all the states.

## Key Terms

**Federalists** supporters of the Constitution

**Antifederalists** opponents of the Constitution

**Publius** the pen name used by Alexander Hamilton, James Madison, and John Jay in a series of articles defending the Constitution

*Federalist Papers* essays written by Alexander Hamilton, James Madison, and John Jay to defend the Constitution

**Bill of Rights** a series of 10 amendments to the Constitution ratified by the states that protect such rights as freedom of speech, press, and religion, as well as due process protections

## Taking Notes

As you read, take notes on the ratification debate. Record your notes in the graphic organizer below.

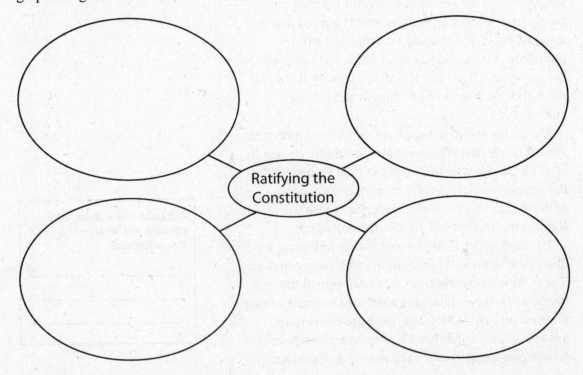

Ratifying the Constitution

# Section Summary

## ANTIFEDERALISTS VERSUS FEDERALISTS

The Framers were aware that the existing Congress and state legislatures would not be happy with the new, stronger national government they were proposing. Therefore, they had included a process for ratifying the Constitution that would bypass both groups, instead calling for voters to elect representatives to a state ratifying convention. The Constitution would become law once 9 of the 13 states ratified it.

The battle for ratification involved the **Antifederalists**, the opponents of the Constitution, and **Federalists**, the supporters of the Constitution. Antifederalists claimed that the national government proposed by the Constitution would become too strong and threaten republicanism and state sovereignty. They also criticized the absence of a bill of rights, without which they feared the new national government could violate personal civil liberties with no fear of punishment. Federalists countered that a sufficiently powerful national government would strengthen the union of the states and have the power to defend the nation against foreign enemies, regulate trade, and control internal disturbances like the earlier Shays's Rebellion. Federalists also highlighted how the separation of powers officially limited federal power.

> **What arguments did Antifederalists make against ratifying the Constitution?**
> _____
> _____

## THE FEDERALIST PAPERS

In order to summon more support for ratification, prominent Federalists James Madison, Alexander Hamilton, and John Jay, under the pen name **Publius**, wrote the *Federalist Papers*, a series of articles defending the Constitution for New York newspapers. The 85 articles—each of which discussed principles underlying the Constitution, such as checks and balances—were collected into a single volume of essays and widely circulated, strongly influencing the ratification debate. Antifederalists responded with essays of their own that frequently addressed the importance of liberty and the guarantee of "unalienable and fundamental rights."

> **What was the point of the *Federalist Papers*?**
> _____
> _____

## THE FIGHT FOR RATIFICATION

The Federalists had been better prepared for the fight over ratification than the Antifederalists, quickly pointing out to small states that they would have equal representation in the Senate, despite their small populations. Yet Federalists found the largest and most powerful states difficult to persuade. Federalists finally agreed to the Antifederalists' demand for a bill of rights. This change had a remarkable effect on ratification. On June 21, 1788, the ninth state ratified the Constitution, and the remaining 4 states ratified it shortly thereafter.

Once the first Congress met, James Madison emphasized that the promised bill of rights should be proposed and ratified quickly. Madison suggested a number of amendments, or changes to the Constitution, that reflected earlier declarations of rights, including the English Bill of Rights and the Declaration of Independence. In September 1789, Congress sent 12 amendments to the states for ratification. By December 1791, the states had ratified 10 of the amendments. Traditionally called the **Bill of Rights**, these 10 amendments protect a number of civil liberties and civil rights, including the freedom of speech, press, and religion.

> **How was the Bill of Rights added to the Constitution?**
> _____
> _____

# The Constitution

## Chapter Summary

**COMPREHENSION AND CRITICAL THINKING**

Use information from the graphic organizer to answer the following
questions.

1. **Define** What are the main goals of the Constitution?

    _____

    _____

2. **Explain** Why is the amendment process important to the Constitution's endurance,
   or its ability to hold up over time?

    _____

    _____

3. **Elaborate** One goal the Framers had for the new government was to promote the
   general welfare. Which principle of the Constitution do you think would most help
   them meet this goal? Explain.

    _____

    _____

## The Constitution

**MAIN IDEA**
Drawing lessons from history, the Framers wrote a constitution that divided, limited, and balanced power among three branches of government.

# Key Terms

**popular sovereignty** concept that a government gets its power from the people and that ultimate political power remains with the people

**limited government** principle that the powers and functions of government are restricted by the U.S. Constitution and other laws

**rule of law** concept that every member of society, including the ruler and government, must obey the law and is never above it

**separation of powers** principle that the duties of governing are divided among the legislative, executive, and judicial branches

**checks and balances** system that gives each branch of government the power to change, reverse, or cancel acts of another branch

**veto** president's power to reject legislation

**judicial review** power to declare legislative and executive acts unconstitutional

**unconstitutional** found to violate any part of the Constitution

**federalism** principle that powers of government are distributed between the national government and the state governments

# Taking Notes

As you read, take notes on the principles of government set out in the Constitution. Record your notes in the graphic organizer below.

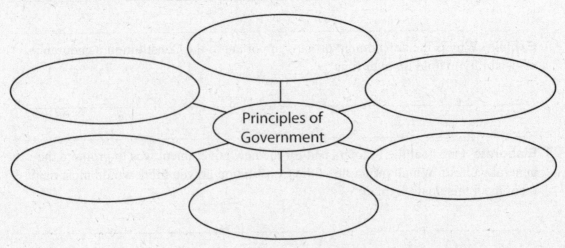

Principles of Government

## Section Summary

### GOALS OF THE CONSTITUTION

As they wrote the Constitution, the Framers had six definite goals for the new national government: form a more perfect union; establish justice, or laws; insure domestic tranquility, or national peace; provide for the common defense of the country; promote the general welfare of states and citizens; and secure the blessings of liberties won by fighting the American Revolution.

Although they knew what the government had to do, the Framers were at first uncertain of how to create the government itself. They knew from recent experience what could happen when a government suppressed the natural rights of its citizens. But the Framers also knew that citizens needed certain laws for the new nation to survive. A strong national government would be able to enforce these laws.

> **What were the Framers afraid would happen if they designed a national government that was too powerful?**
>
> _____
>
> _____

### PRINCIPLES OF GOVERNMENT IN THE CONSTITUTION

The Framers solved their dilemma over the balance of power by drawing upon six basic principles of governing: popular sovereignty, limited government, separation of powers, checks and balances, judicial review, and federalism. These principles ensure that the government's powers are subject to the will of the people and are presented in general terms throughout the Preamble, seven Articles, and 27 Amendments of the Constitution.

### POPULAR SOVEREIGNTY

**Popular sovereignty** is the idea that a government gets it powers from the people it governs. The Framers began the Constitution with this idea: "We the People of the United States…do ordain and establish this Constitution…" Today, people participate in popular sovereignty in every election, when they choose and vote for the citizens they wish to lead their community, state, or country.

> **How is voting a good example of popular sovereignty?**
>
> _____
>
> _____

### LIMITED GOVERNMENT

**Limited government** is the idea that the powers of government are restricted by the U.S. Constitution and

other laws. This idea follows the concept of the
**rule of law**, which means that everyone in the country,
from everyday citizens to the president, is subject to the
same laws. Although you will find many examples of
the government's powers throughout the Constitution,
such as the power to declare war or collect taxes, you
will also find examples of how these powers are limited.

> **Why was it important to the Framers that government officials follow the same laws as all other Americans?**
>
> _____
>
> _____

## SEPARATION OF POWERS

The Framers included the **separation of powers**
within the Constitution by assigning specific
responsibilities to the three branches of government:
legislative (Congress), executive (president), and
judicial (Supreme Court).

## CHECKS AND BALANCES

By separating powers, the Framers also guaranteed a
system of **checks and balances** that applies to all
three branches. For example, by giving the president
the power to **veto** legislation passed by Congress, the
Framers made it possible for the executive branch to
check the power of Congress. Yet, Congress can
override a veto if it has enough votes, checking one of
the executive branch's powers. Likewise, the Supreme
Court and other federal courts can declare legislation
unconstitutional—but the president gets to nominate
and Congress gets to approve all judges.

> **What is one way the judicial branch can check the legislative branch? What is one way the legislative branch can check the executive branch?**
>
> _____
>
> _____

## JUDICIAL REVIEW

The federal courts have the very important power of
**judicial review**, although that power is only implied
in the Constitution. This power allows the courts to
determine if a law or other government action is
**unconstitutional**, or violates the Constitution.

## FEDERALISM

The final principle the Framers built the Constitution
upon is **federalism**, or a system in which a
government's power is divided between the national
government and state governments. The Tenth
Amendment to the Constitution was passed in order to
clarify those powers that belong to the federal
government and those that belong to the states.

> **Why was the Tenth Amendment necessary?**
>
> _____
>
> _____

## The Constitution

**MAIN IDEA**
The Constitution is both a product of its time and a document for all time. It can be changed as society's needs change.

# Key Terms

**supermajority** any majority that is larger than a simple majority, such as three-fifths, two-thirds, or three-fourths

**repeal** cancel or revoke a law by a legislative act

# Taking Notes

As you read, take notes on the amendment process. Record your notes in the chart below.

| Proposing | Ratifying |
|-----------|-----------|
| 1. | 1. |
| 2. | 2. |

# Section Summary

## JEFFERSON AND MADISON ON AMENDING THE CONSTITUTION

Thomas Jefferson and James Madison had different views on whether it should be possible to amend the Constitution. Jefferson believed that an amendment process was necessary, since future generations would need to modify laws as society changed. Madison argued that the ability to change the Constitution would take away its authority. Madison also was worried that, if the process for changing the Constitution was made too easy, political groups would change the document to meet their own needs.

> What adjective could you use to describe Jefferson's view on amending the Constitution? What about Madison's view?
>
> _____
>
> _____

## A DOCUMENT FOR ALL TIME

The Constitution the Framers wrote has needed to be amended over the years—but only a few times. Many of these amendments have corrected injustices in the original document. For example, original compromises allowing slavery and prohibitions on who was permitted to vote were some of the first sections of the Constitution to be amended. Americans' ability to amend their Constitution helps the document remain relevant for each generation.

## THE AMENDMENT PROCESS

Article V describes the amendment process. The Framers purposely designed this process so that it would be complicated enough to discourage factions from making changes that did not represent the needs of most Americans.

Every amendment must first be proposed, in one of two ways. Either a **supermajority**—a majority larger than a simple majority—of Congress (at least two-thirds of the House and two-thirds of the Senate) or a national convention called by at least two-thirds of the state legislatures may propose the amendment. Due to uncertainty over the wording of Article V, all existing amendments have been proposed by Congress

The amendment then needs to be ratified. This can also happen in one of two ways. Three-fourths of state legislatures can vote to ratify, sometimes after first calling citizens to cast an advisory vote. Alternatively,

> Explain two different ways an amendment could be proposed and ratified.
>
> _____
>
> _____

elected delegates at state conventions called by at least three-fourths of the states can vote to ratify the proposed amendment.

Amendments, like other sections of the Constitution, can also be amended. To **repeal**, or revoke, an amendment, another amendment must be proposed and ratified. One example of this is the Twenty-First Amendment, which was ratified in order to repeal the Eighteenth Amendment of the Constitution.

> **Why is it logical that a new amendment is needed to repeal an earlier amendment?**
>
> _____
>
> _____

## MORE THAN 200 YEARS OF AMENDMENTS

Twenty-seven amendments have been added to the Constitution. The first 10 comprise the Bill of Rights, which was added almost immediately after the Constitution itself was ratified. These amendments protect Americans' personal freedoms and liberties, including freedom of speech and religion, the right to bear arms, and the right to a speedy trial. The later amendments in the Bill of Rights further protect individual rights by preventing the government from taking away any of them—or those belonging to the individual states.

The 17 other amendments were added over the next 200 years and reflected changes in American society. Among these are a series of amendments banning slavery and recognizing the rights of African Americans—passed shortly after the end of the Civil War—as well as amendments that allow the popular election of senators and give women the right to vote. Every amendment is proof of how the Constitution makes it possible for Americans to have a flexible government.

> **How does an amendment that changes voting laws reflect changes in American society?**
>
> _____
>
> _____
>
> _____

## The Constitution

 **MAIN IDEA**
The scope and impact of the Constitution have expanded as it has been put into practice, interpreted, and applied to new or changing social and political challenges.

# Key Terms

**executive agreements** arrangements or compacts with foreign leaders or foreign governments

**political party** an organized group that seeks to win elections in order to influence the activities of government

**cabinet** a group of advisers consisting of the heads of the executive departments

**gridlock** inability to govern effectively due to separation of powers

**electoral college** body of 538 people elected from the 50 states and the District of Columbia who elect the president and vice president

# Taking Notes

As you read, take notes on how the reach of the Constitution has expanded. Record your notes in the graphic organizer below.

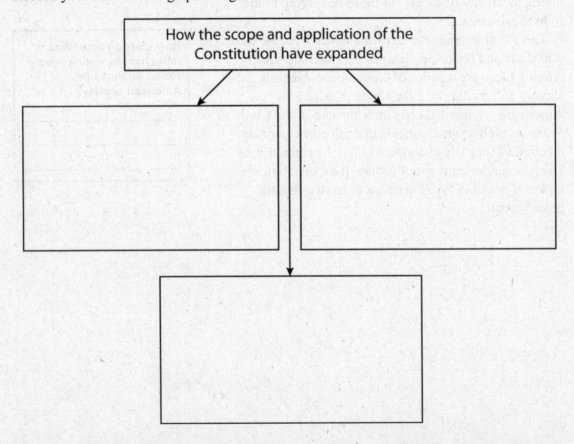

How the scope and application of the Constitution have expanded

# Section Summary

## THE FEDERAL GOVERNMENT APPLIES THE CONSTITUTION

Over the years, each branch of government has applied and thereby expanded the meaning of the Constitution—and the scope of government itself. The legislative branch, using powers it has interpreted in the Constitution, has increased the lower level of the judicial branch, created various executive departments and agencies, and passed legislation that often requires a new way of looking at old laws. The executive branch has interpreted the Constitution in other ways to make **executive agreements**— arrangements with foreign countries—and adopt rules for its departments and agencies.

    The judicial branch's interpretation has resulted in court rulings that apply laws to modern-day situations. This power of judicial review is often the subject of the debate over "loose" versus "strict" construction of the Constitution. Some Americans believe that it is possible to infer other concepts beyond what the actual words in the document say—this is loose construction. Other Americans believe that the powers of the Constitution lie in the literal meaning of its words—this is strict construction.

> **Give two examples of how the legislative branch has interpreted the Constitution.**
>
> _____
> _____
> _____
> _____

> **Why do you think judicial review is often a controversial subject in politics?**
>
> _____
> _____

## POLITICAL PARTIES, CUSTOMS, AND TRADITIONS

In addition to the three branches, other groups also influence how the Constitution is interpreted. For example, **political parties**, or groups who wish to win elections in order to influence government, can have a great effect on candidates, the kind of legislation Congress passes, and who a president nominates to become federal judges. Other groups, including political action committees and political bloggers, also affect legislation by making their voices heard— sometimes with the help of a political party and sometimes without.

    Customs and traditions also play a role in how government is carried out. For example, George Washington created his **cabinet**—a group of advisers consisting of the heads of the executive departments— through an interpretation of Article II of the

> **What do you think the relationship is between a political party and its candidates? Underline evidence for your answer in the paragraph at left.**
>
> _____
> _____

Constitution. Since then, every U.S. president has created a cabinet. Other traditions have become formal law, as in the case of the Twenty-second Amendment. Although earlier presidents had all served a maximum of two terms in office, President Franklin D. Roosevelt served four terms. In response to this break from tradition, Congress passed the Twenty-second Amendment, which limited presidents to two terms.

## CRITICISMS OF THE CONSTITUTION

While the U.S. Constitution is one of the most respected documents in the world, it is criticized for various reasons. Some criticize the **gridlock**, or inability to govern, that can take place due to separation of powers. These critics feel that it is too easy for one branch to blame another when certain policy-making cannot be accomplished. Others believe that the Constitution does not allow for fair representation in Congress, arguing that states with much larger populations should be given more senators.

> **Why do some people criticize how states are represented in the Senate?**
>
> _____
>
> _____

Additional criticisms involve the effectiveness of the **electoral college**—the body of people from the 50 states and the District of Columbia who elect the president and vice president—and winner-take-all elections. In both cases, critics worry that large portions of the popular vote do not hold enough value.

# Federalism

## Chapter Summary

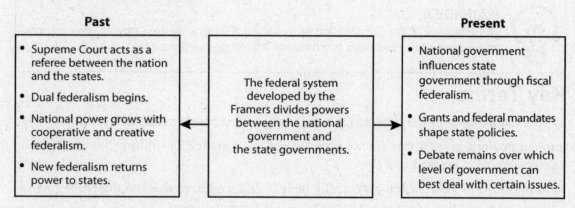

**Past**

- Supreme Court acts as a referee between the nation and the states.
- Dual federalism begins.
- National power grows with cooperative and creative federalism.
- New federalism returns power to states.

The federal system developed by the Framers divides powers between the national government and the state governments.

**Present**

- National government influences state government through fiscal federalism.
- Grants and federal mandates shape state policies.
- Debate remains over which level of government can best deal with certain issues.

## COMPREHENSION AND CRITICAL THINKING

Use information from the graphic organizer to answer the following questions.

1. **Identify** How does the national government influence state policy today?

   _____

   _____

2. **Analyze** What type of national event might have inspired the shift from dual federalism to a system in which the national government grew more powerful?

   _____

   _____

3. **Develop** Why do you think some policymakers wished to return authority to the state governments during the period of new federalism? What might they have been hoping to change?

   _____

   _____

   _____

# Federalism

**MAIN IDEA**
The Framers of the Constitution established a federal system that divides powers and responsibility between the national and state governments.

## Key Terms

**expressed powers**  powers granted to the national government by the Constitution

**implied powers**  powers that are not specifically listed in the Constitution but are logical extensions of expressed powers

**inherent powers**  powers that historically have been recognized as naturally belonging to all governments that conduct the business of a sovereign nation

**reserved powers**  powers that belong to the states because the Constitution neither delegates these powers to the national government nor prohibits them to the states

**concurrent powers**  powers held by the national government and the state governments at the same time

**full faith and credit clause**  Article IV of the Constitution, which requires that states give "full faith and credit" to the public acts, official records, and judicial proceedings of every other state

## Taking Notes

As you read, take notes on the powers of the national, state, and shared powers. Record your notes in the graphic organizer below.

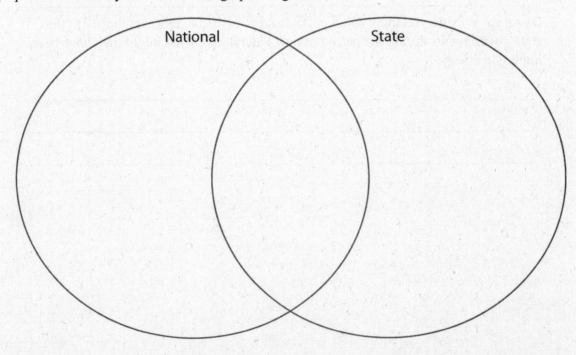

National   State

# Section Summary

## WHY FEDERALISM?

When the Framers met at the Constitutional Convention, they knew they needed to design a stronger national government, yet avoid the dangers of a unitary system. The biggest challenge was to balance this powerful national government with states' rights and still ensure a republican government. The Framers met this challenge in the Constitution, which divides powers between two levels of government: state and national. In this federal-style government, the national government was granted all powers having to do with the states' best interests and the state governments were granted all other powers.

> **How did the Framers decide which powers to give the states?**
> _____
> _____

## NATIONAL POWERS

The Constitution grants the national government and each of its branches specific powers, known as **expressed powers** or enumerated powers. The national government also has **implied powers**, or powers that are not specifically listed in the Constitution but are logical extensions of expressed powers. Finally, the national government possesses **inherent powers**—powers that historically have been recognized as naturally belonging to all governments that conduct the business of a sovereign nation.

> **What is the difference between expressed powers and implied and inherent powers?**
> _____
> _____
> _____

## STATE POWERS

Per a clause in the Bill of Rights, states have **reserved powers**—powers that belong to the states because the Constitution neither delegates those powers to the national government nor denies them to the states. States use this authority to regulate health, public safety, and general welfare, from controlling public school systems to enforcing criminal laws.

## SHARED POWERS

Powers held by the national government and the state governments at the same time are called **concurrent powers**. Although Article VI of the Constitution—known as the supremacy clause—states that the Constitution and national laws and treaties are the supreme law of the land, states may also exercise any power not given *exclusively* to the national government, such as the power to collect taxes.

## THE LIMITS OF POWER

The Constitution denies certain powers to both the national and state governments. Among other limits on its power, the national government cannot tax exports between states, spend money unless authorized by Congress, exercise powers reserved to the states, or interfere with basic liberties. The states are also denied specific powers, including the power to coin money or enter into treaties. Both levels of government are denied some of the same powers, such as denying a citizen the right to a trial by jury or passing ex post facto laws.

> **Give an example of one power denied to the national government. Then give one example of a power denied to the states.**
>
> _____
>
> _____
>
> _____

## NATION AND STATE RELATIONS

The Constitution also sets guidelines for relationships between states and between states and the national government. The national government may only recognize representative or republican state governments, and is responsible for protecting the states from foreign invasions and domestic uprisings. Additionally, the national government must grant states equal representation in the Senate and levy taxes equally across states, and is prohibited from splitting up states or changing state boundaries.

The Constitution encourages cooperation among states, and although state laws vary, it requires states to extradite a person charged with a crime to the state in which the crime occurred for prosecution. To ease extradition and other processes, the **full faith and credit clause**, or Article IV, requires that states give "full faith and credit" to the public acts, official records, and judicial proceedings of every other state. Also, the privileges and immunity clause prevents most circumstances in which a person from one state may be discriminated against by another state.

The Constitution says nothing about local governments, and so those are created and reorganized by the state government. The only provision, which concerns Native American nations, simply authorizes the national government to make treaties with these nations.

> **What does the privileges and immunity clause prohibit?**
>
> _____
>
> _____

## Federalism

**MAIN IDEA**
Over the past 200 years, conflicts over the balance of power between the
national and state governments have led to different trends in federalism.

# Key Terms

**dual federalism**  a system of federalism in which both state and national governments
were equal authorities operating within their own spheres of influence, as defined by a
strict reading of the Constitution

**doctrine of nullification**  the idea that states had the right to cancel national laws that they
believed contradicted or clashed with state interests

**doctrine of secession**  the idea that states had the right to separate themselves from the
Union

**cooperative federalism**  a system of federalism under the New Deal in which the national
and state governments worked together to meet a crisis

**creative federalism**  a system of federalism under President Lyndon Johnson in which the
national government released grants to state and local communities to achieve national
goals

**new federalism**  a system of federalism in which authority is returned to the state
governments

**devolution**  the idea of returning power to states

# Taking Notes

As you read, take notes on the people and events that led to changes in
American federalism. Record your notes in the graphic organizer below.

```
┌─────────────────────────────────────────────────────┐
│                                                       │
│                                                       │
│                                                       │
└─────────────────────────────────────────────────────┘
                          │
                          ▼
┌─────────────────────────────────────────────────────┐
│                                                       │
│                                                       │
│                                                       │
└─────────────────────────────────────────────────────┘
                          │
                          ▼
┌─────────────────────────────────────────────────────┐
│                                                       │
│                                                       │
│                                                       │
└─────────────────────────────────────────────────────┘
```

# Section Summary

## ROLE OF THE SUPREME COURT

The Framers of the Constitution were aware that the system of federalism would eventually lead to conflicts between the national and state governments. They disagreed over which level of government should have more power and so addressed that decision indirectly. In Article III of the Constitution, the Supreme Court is given the power to act as referee by hearing cases involving the Constitution, U.S. laws, and disputes between states. The Framers also included Article VI, or the supremacy clause, which states that the Constitution and national laws and treaties are "the supreme law of the land."

| Who referees disputes between states? |
| --- |
| _____ |

## DUAL FEDERALISM

The United States first followed a system of **dual federalism**, under which both state and national governments were equal authorities operating within their own spheres of influence. The national government used the powers assigned to it in the Constitution and the states exercised all other powers, per the Tenth Amendment. This form of federalism lasted from about 1789 to the 1930s, first coming into national debate in a dispute over whether the national government had the authority to establish a national bank. In *McCulloch* v. *Maryland* (1819), the Supreme Court ruled that the Constitution's necessary and proper clause gave the national government the power to take actions necessary and proper to carrying out its expressed powers, in this case starting a national bank to regulate commerce and currency.

| In *McCulloch* v. *Maryland*, why did the Supreme Court rule that the government had the power to establish a national bank? |
| --- |
| _____ |
| _____ |
| _____ |
| _____ |

In the tense years leading up to and during the Civil War, the struggle between states' rights and national power intensified. Southern states proclaimed their belief in the **doctrine of nullification**, the idea that states had the right to nullify, or cancel, national laws that they believed contradicted or clashed with state interests. Under the doctrine, if a state did vote to nullify a law, three-quarters of the other states would then have to ratify an amendment to enact the law; the original state could then follow the law or secede. This latter action fell under the **doctrine of secession**, the idea that states had the right to separate themselves from the Union. South Carolina did nullify a law in 1832, and 11 southern states seceded from the Union at the start of the Civil War in 1861. Yet the outcome of the war resolved that states could *not* secede from the Union when they disagreed with its policies, as well as broadened the national government's power, exemplified by the passage of the Reconstruction Amendments.

## EXPANDING NATIONAL POWER

The national government's power continued to increase into the twentieth century, as states became unable to handle all of the social and economic issues that accompanied a huge influx of immigrants and technology. Congress passed several pieces of important legislation, including bills to regulate the now-mammoth railroad industry's rates and to prevent monopolies and encourage competition.

During the Great Depression, national power expanded yet again under President Franklin Roosevelt's New Deal programs, although the states worked hand-in-hand with federal policymakers to address the crisis—a form of federalism called **cooperative federalism**. In the 1960s, under President Lyndon Johnson, this system transformed into **creative federalism**—a system of federalism in which the national government released grants to state and local communities to achieve national goals. Johnson's Great Society plan convinced states to address poverty and social inequality by withholding funding if states did not cooperate.

> **Explain creative federalism in your own words.**
> _____
> _____
> _____
> _____

## NEW FEDERALISM

President Ronald Reagan took office at the beginning of the 1980s and immediately carried through on a promise to return authority to the state governments, a system now known as **new federalism**. President Reagan believed that the states were better equipped to deal with citizens' needs than the national government and adjusted federal grants accordingly. In the 1990s, the Republican Party also promised to scale down federal spending and return power to the states, a concept known as **devolution**.

> **What was the purpose of new federalism?**
> _____
> _____

## Federalism

**MAIN IDEA**
Today, the balance of power between the states and the national government is characterized by a system of grants and mandates, as well as by a number of key policy areas.

## Key Terms

**fiscal federalism** a system of spending, taxing, and providing aid in the federal system

**grants-in-aid** money and other resources that the national government provides to pay for state and local activities

**categorical grant** a federal grant that can only be used for a specific purpose, or category, of state and local spending

**block grant** a federal grant that is given for general purposes or for broad policy areas

**federal mandates** demands on a state to carry out certain policies as a condition of receiving grant money

## Taking Notes

As you read, take notes on the features of present-day federalism. Record your notes in the graphic organizer below.

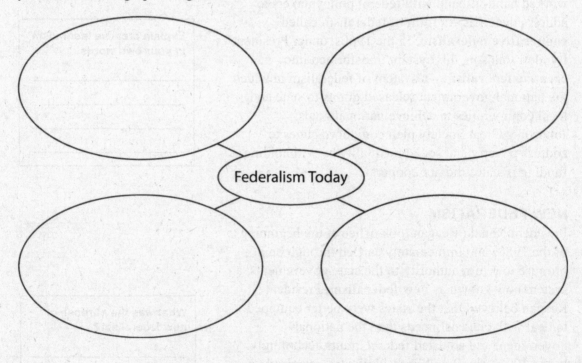

Federalism Today

# Section Summary

## FISCAL FEDERALISM

Today the national government influences state policies—and its own priorities—through **fiscal federalism**, a system of spending, taxing, and providing aid in the federal system. The national government has been assisting states as far back as the Articles of Confederation, often giving states grants of land to sell or do with as they like. In the twentieth century, the national government's power increased with the use of **grants-in-aid**—money and other resources that the national government provides to pay for state and local activities, ranging from low-income housing to disaster preparedness programs. These grants are funded by federal income taxes.

> **What makes up the system of fiscal federalism?**
> _____
> _____
> _____

## GRANTS AND MANDATES

The national government frequently uses **categorical grants**, or federal grants that can only be used for a specific purpose, or category, of state and local spending, to give aid to states. These kinds of grants can fund a variety of programs, from the construction of a new airport to relief efforts in a region affected by a natural disaster. States are often expected to also contribute money toward the project being funded, and the quantity of the categorical grant may depend on the state's population.

**Block grants** are federal grants that are given for more general purposes than a categorical grant or for broad policy areas, such as welfare or education. States can spend the money as they see fit. When the era of new federalism began in the 1980s, many categorical grants were changed to block grants.

Federal mandates are the third way the national government gives monetary aid to states. Leaving much less spending control to the states than categorical or block grants do, **federal mandates** are demands to carry out certain policies as a condition of receiving grant money. In the past, the mandates have been applied—and justified by the equal protection clause of the Fourteenth Amendment—to establish affirmative action and certain environmental regulations, including the Clean Air Act of 1970. States who do not meet the demands of a mandate

> **What is the main difference between block grants and federal mandates?**
> _____
> _____
> _____
> _____

may lose the funding. Additionally, some federal mandates are unfunded—a source of contention between the two levels of government.

## ISSUES IN FEDERALISM TODAY

Federalism is at the center of many national debates today. One such debate involves welfare systems, over which the states have had control through federal block grants since 1996. Although the number of people on welfare decreased for several years, some people argue that this was due to to a strong economy. Others say it was the flexibility gained when control was passed to the state level. While the number of Americans on welfare remained steady from 2001-2007, an economic downturn made numbers rise again.

The environment is another source of conflict between the national and state governments. While protecting the environment has traditionally been the responsibility of the national government, many Americans believe that state and local governments are better be able to address environmental issues, as they are familiar with regional needs and threats.

While states have assumed many costs of immigration-related issues, Americans are turning to their state and national governments for solutions to rising health care costs. To help address the problem, the national government passed the Affordable Care Act in 2010. The law, also called Obamacare, provided all Americans with new benefits and some with subsidies to help pay for health insurance.

> **According to supporters, why would it be better to address environmental issues at the state level?**
>
> _____
>
> _____
>
> _____
>
> _____

**Congress: The Legislative Branch**

# Chapter Summary

The Constitution both defines and limits the powers of Congress.

In the Senate, each state is represented equally. Today's Senate has 100 members—two senators from each of the 50 states.

Congress is the branch of government that makes laws. It is divided into two houses, the House of Representatives and the Senate.

The House of Representatives is the more representative house of Congress. Representation in the House is based on a state's population.

The main job of Congress is to make laws. To become a law, a bill goes through a multistage process involving both houses of Congress and approval by the president.

## COMPREHENSION AND CRITICAL THINKING
Use information from the graphic organizer to answer the following questions.

1. **Describe** What is the source of Congress's power?

    _____

    _____

2. **Compare** How does representation in the House of Representatives compare to representation in the Senate?

    _____

    _____

3. **Evaluate** What is your opinion about the Framers' decision to limit the powers of Congress?

    _____

    _____

## Congress: The Legislative Branch

**MAIN IDEA**
The voters elect members of Congress to represent them and to enact laws in their name. Congress plays a vital role in our government's system of checks and balances

## Key Terms

**constituents** the people who live within the particular geographic area a member of Congress represents

**apportionment** the distribution of House seats among the states based on population

**appropriation** a bill that sets aside funds for a specific purpose

**impeachment** when Congress charges an official in the executive or judicial branch with wrongdoing and brings them to trial

**oversight** when Congress uses its broad powers to review how the executive branch is operating and to make sure it is following the laws Congress has passed

## Taking Notes

As you read, take notes on the powers and features of Congress. Record your notes in the graphic organizer below.

| Representing the People | Structure | Checks and Balances |
|---|---|---|
|  |  |  |

# Section Summary

## CONGRESS AND THE PEOPLE

Although the people hold sovereign power in the system of American government, they elect representatives to make and carry out laws. Therefore, Congress is the body through which the will of the people becomes law.

Members of Congress represent the people in different ways. First, each member is responsible for representing the often conflicting needs and interests of his or her **constituents**—the people who live within the particular geographic area he or she represents. Second, a member of Congress must balance the demands of various interest groups—organized groups of like-minded people who join together to influence government and its policies—with the need to represent everyone fairly, even though interest groups typically include only a small number of the member's constituents. Finally, a member of Congress must consider the needs of the country as a whole. To do this, the member may sometimes need to serve his or her constituents directly and sometimes need to vote for legislation that benefits the country at large, not just his or her constituency.

Members of Congress share some personal characteristics. The average age of members is mid- to upper fifties. Most members are wealthier than the general population. Also, most members are white men, although gender and racial diversity has increased in recent years.

> **What different groups does a member of Congress represent?**
>
> _____
>
> _____

## THE STRUCTURE OF CONGRESS

Congress is a bicameral legislature whose two houses are the House of Representatives and the Senate.

In the House, the process of **apportionment** is how seats are distributed among the states based on population. Each House seat is meant to represent about the same number of people; therefore, larger states have more representatives. The total number of House seats is fixed by law at 435, and all members serve two-year terms that are contested at the same time.

In the Senate, there are two members per state, for a total of 100 senators. While the Constitution originally

> **What is the purpose of apportionment?**
>
> _____
>
> _____

gave the state legislatures the power to elect senators, members of the Senate are now elected by the people for six-year terms. The terms are staggered so that every two years one-third of senators are up for election.

The delegates at the Constitutional Convention chose a bicameral design for Congress as part of the Great Compromise—an agreement to settle the fierce debate over how state population should affect representation. A bicameral legislature allowed one house in which small and large states had equal representation and one house in which representation was based on population. The final design also settled a debate over which members of Congress should be directly elected: Until 1913, members of the House were popularly elected, but senators were not.

> **Which house of Congress gives small and large states equal representation?**
>
> _____

## CONGRESS AND CHECKS AND BALANCES

There are several ways Congress can check the other two branches. With few limits, Congress can deny federal spending with which it disagrees by refusing to enact an **appropriation**—a bill that sets aside funds for a specific purpose. Congress can also refuse to approve treaties the president has made with foreign governments and reject presidential appointees, such as potential Supreme Court justices.

Congress also has the power to impeach officials in both other branches. **Impeachment** involves charging an official with wrongdoing and bringing them to trial, where, if convicted, they can be removed from office. The House of Representatives begins the process by drawing up and voting to approve charges. The Senate then holds a trial, at which the vice president—or in some cases, the Chief Justice of the Supreme Court—serves as judge. A two-thirds vote by the Senate is required to remove a person from office.

> **Why is impeachment an important power?**
>
> _____
>
> _____

Congress can further check the judicial branch by starting the process of amending the Constitution, possibly limiting the courts' power to declare certain legislation unconstitutional. Additional checks on the executive branch include voting to override a veto and conducting congressional **oversight**, or checking up on how the executive branch is operating and whether it is following laws Congress has passed.

## Congress: The Legislative Branch

**MAIN IDEA**
The Constitution gives Congress many expressed powers, and it implies some others. The Constitution also places limits on the powers of Congress.

# Key Terms

**necessary and proper clause** Article I, Section 8, Clause 18 of the Constitution, which states Congress's implied powers; also called the elastic clause

**indirect tax** a tax levied on one person but passed on to another for payment to the government

**direct tax** a tax an individual pays directly to the government

**deficit** when the federal government is not generating enough income to meet its expenses

**commerce clause** Article I, Section 8, Clause 3 of the Constitution, which states that the federal government has the right to regulate interstate commerce

**subpoenas** legal documents that require a person to testify in a certain matter

**writ of habeas corpus** a court order that forces the police to present a person in court to face charges, except in cases of rebellion or invasion

**bill of attainder** a law that punishes a person without a trial

**ex post facto laws** laws that criminalize an action that took place in the past and was legal at the time

# Taking Notes

As you read, take notes on the powers of Congress. Record your notes in the graphic organizer below.

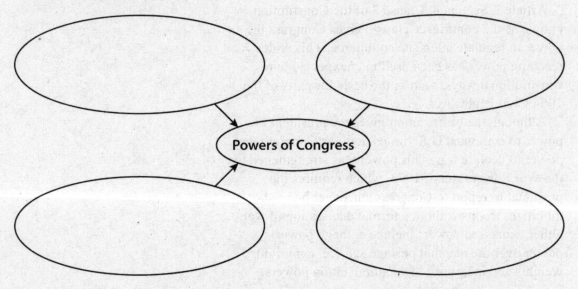

# Section Summary

## DEFINING THE POWERS OF CONGRESS

Article I, Section 8, lists specific, or expressed, powers, of Congress. Clause 18 of the same section, known as the **necessary and proper clause** or the elastic clause, suggests that Congress also has implied powers to "make all laws that are necessary and proper" for executing government. Additionally, Americans assume that Congress—and the other branches—have inherent powers, or those that all governments of independent nations possess. Finally, there are some powers explicitly denied Congress.

> How are Congress's implied powers different from its expressed powers?
> _____
> _____

## EXPRESSED POWERS OF CONGRESS

The expressed powers of Congress mainly fall into three categories: financing, commerce, and defense.

Congress's financial powers involve the power to levy taxes and borrow money. Until the Sixteenth Amendment gave Congress the power to levy an income tax, most revenue was collected through **indirect taxes**, or taxes levied on one person but passed on to another for payment to the government. Today, revenue from income taxes—an example of a **direct tax**, or a tax an individual pays directly to the government—far exceeds that of indirect taxes. Congress also borrows money to allow the government to function even when there is not enough revenue to cover spending—a situation known as a budget **deficit**.

> How does Congress collect most revenue today: direct taxes or indirect taxes?
> _____

Article I, Section 8, Clause 3 of the Constitution, known as the **commerce clause**, gives Congress the power to regulate interstate commerce. This wide-reaching power has been used in unexpected but constitutional ways, such as the basis for parts of the 1964 Civil Rights Act.

Although the Constitution gives the president the power to command U.S. troops, it gives Congress the power to declare war. This power was strengthened by the War Powers Act of 1973, which requires the president to report to Congress whenever he or she mobilizes troops without a formal declaration of war. Other expressed powers include coinage power; power over the national postage service, copyrights, weights and measures; and naturalization powers.

## IMPLIED POWERS OF CONGRESS

The necessary and proper clause gives Congress implied powers it may need to carry out its expressed powers. For years, politicians have debated how loosely or strictly this part of the Constitution should be applied, and how extensively congress should be able to apply the clause to expand its national power.

## NONLEGISLATIVE POWERS

Congress has some nonlegislative powers. Both houses can propose amendments to the Constitution, conduct investigations—sometimes issuing **subpoenas**, legal documents that require a person to testify in a certain matter—contribute to impeachments, and confirm replacements if the vice presidency is vacant. The House alone can choose a president or vice president if no candidate receives a majority of votes in the electoral college. The Senate alone can choose a vice president in the same situation, as well as advise on and approve presidential appointees and treaties.

> **If you receive a subpoena, what must you do?**
> _____

## LIMITS ON THE POWERS OF CONGRESS

Congress's powers are limited by the system of checks and balances. Article I, Section 9 also denies Congress specific powers, such as the power to suspend the **writ of habeas corpus**, a court order that forces the police to present a person in court to face charges, except in cases of rebellion or invasion. Furthermore, Congress cannot pass **bills of attainder**, laws that punish a person without a trial, or **ex post facto laws**, laws that criminalize an action that took place in the past and was legal at the time.

> **Name two things Congress cannot do.**
> _____
> _____

## THE CHANGING POWER OF CONGRESS

The power of Congress has grown steadily, especially during periods of national crisis or outcry, including the Great Depression and the Civil Rights Era. The relationship between Congress and the president varies, with some presidents allowing Congress to be more aggressive than others.

## Congress: The Legislative Branch

**MAIN IDEA**
The House of Representatives, with its frequent elections and regular reapportionment, is the more representative chamber of Congress. Its members carry out much of their work in committees.

## Key Terms

**reapportionment** the process in which seats are redistributed among states based on the results of the census

**gerrymandering** the practice of drawing district boundaries for political advantage

**Speaker of the House** the most powerful member and the presiding office of the House of Representatives

**bills** proposed laws

**floor leader** elected member of the majority or minority party who helps manage the actions and strategy of the party in the House of Representatives

**whips** elected members of the majority or minority party who encourage fellow party members to vote as the party leadership wants

**party caucus** a meeting of all the House of Representatives members from a particular party

**standing committees** permanent committees in the House of Representatives

**select committees** committees, typically temporary, that carry out specific tasks not already covered by existing committees

**joint committees** committees formed with Senate members that address broad issues affecting both chambers

## Taking Notes

As you read, take notes on the features of the House of Representatives. Record your notes in the graphic organizer below.

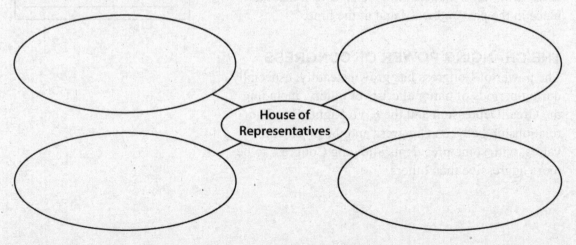

# Section Summary

## MEMBERSHIP IN THE HOUSE

When writing the Constitution, the Framers designed the House of Representatives to be the chamber of Congress more representative of the people. To that end, the Constitution requires slightly less of House members than senators. Representatives in the House must be at least 25 years old, have been a U.S. citizen for at least seven years, and live in the state—and customarily the district—he or she represents. Informally, members typically require an appealing personality to win election in the first place, as well as the means to raise money for expensive campaigns.

There are very few situations in which the House can exclude an elected representative. However, it can expel a sitting member by a two-thirds vote.

> **What three requirements does the Constitution include for members of the House?**
>
> _____
>
> _____

## REAPPORTIONMENT AND REDISTRICTING

The 435 members of Congress represent an average of approximately 735,000 Americans, with a minimum of one representative per state. The process of **reapportionment** ensures that seats are redistributed every 10 years based on census results. In this process, some states may lose seats and others may gain them.

Although Congress is given the responsibility of reapportionment, the state governments control redistricting, or the process of creating district boundaries. Often, the party in power in a state legislature will redraw boundaries for political purposes, a process known as **gerrymandering**. Over the years, the Supreme Court has placed some limits on gerrymandering, ruling the practice of creating districts that include many more people than other districts, or districts drawn to disenfranchise or benefit racial minorities, unconstitutional.

> **How and when does Congress decide to redistribute seats?**
>
> _____
>
> _____

## LEADERSHIP IN THE HOUSE

The Constitution grants the House of Representatives the power to choose its own leaders. The presiding officer of the House and its most powerful member is the **Speaker of the House**. This official is second in the line of succession for the presidency and is elected by the other members, always originating with the majority party. House rules and years of tradition have granted the Speaker the power to preside over debates; give members the authority to speak on the House floor; assign **bills**, or proposed laws to specific committees; schedule if and when a measure comes up for debate and how it is debated; and assign members to different House committees.

Other House officials include elected floor leaders and party whips. Each of the two major parties has a **floor leader**, who helps manage the actions and strategy of the party in the house. The majority party's floor leader assists the Speaker. The minority party's floor leader acts as chief House spokesperson for the party and tries to unify fellow party members on issues. Each party also has a **whip**, whose job it is to encourage fellow party members to vote as the party leadership wishes. The election of floor leaders and whips—as well as the Speaker—take place during **party caucuses**, meetings of all the House members from a particular party.

> **Describe a whip's role in your own words.**
> _____
> _____

Under rules it created, the House can vote to issue a reprimand or a censure against a member. Also, the Rules Committee sets rules for when, how, and under what conditions debate on a bill will take place.

## THE ROLE OF COMMITTEES

The House of Representatives depends on its many committees to gather knowledge on specific issues. There are 20 **standing committees**, or permanent committees, in which there are several more focused subcommittees. The House Committee on Ways and Means is one of the most powerful standing committees, dealing with taxes and other revenue-raising measures. There are also **select committees**, which are typically temporary and carry out tasks not covered by existing committees. **Joint committees** are those that the House forms with the Senate when an issue affects both chambers. Conference committees are the fourth type of committee.

> **What is the difference between standing and select committees?**
> _____
> _____

With some exceptions, House members can serve on up to two standing committees and four subcommittees. Each committee is headed by a chair, who is elected—partially on the basis of seniority—with a six-year term limit.

# Congress: The Legislative Branch

## Section 4

**MAIN IDEA**
Senators represent entire states, have longer terms, and follow different rules of debate. These features help give the Senate its reputation as a more weighty and careful body than the House.

## Key Terms

**president of the Senate**  position assigned to the vice president of the United States by the Constitution that allows the vice president to preside over debates and break tie votes

**president pro tempore**  the person who presides over the Senate in the absence of the president of the Senate

**Senate majority leader**  the most powerful position in the Senate, elected by the majority's party caucus

**seniority rule**  tradition that says the most senior majority senator on a committee becomes committee chair

**filibuster**  when opponents of a measure take control of the Senate floor and refuse to stop talking in an effort to prevent the measure from coming up for a vote

**cloture**  an end to debate

## Taking Notes

As you read, take notes on the features of the Senate. Record your notes in the graphic organizer below.

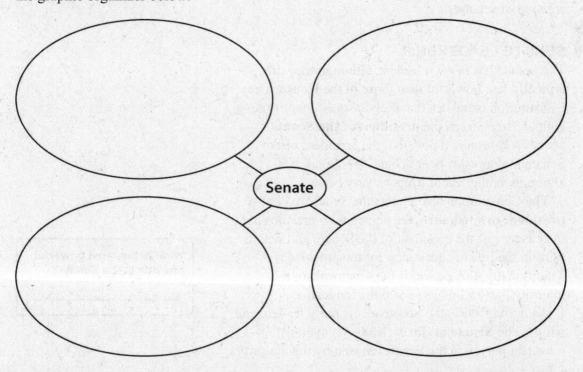

Senate

# Section Summary

## THE SENATE AND ITS MEMBERSHIP

The Senate is also known as the upper house, an alternate name that indicates the prestige of the chamber and its special powers. Senators are typically national figures, since there are so few of them and each must win statewide, as opposed to district-wide, election.

The constitutional requirements for senators are somewhat more stringent than those for members of the House of Representatives. A senator must be at least 30 years old, have been a U.S. citizen for at least nine years, and live in the state he or she represents. Informally, most senators are white men, older and wealthier than their colleagues in the House.

Senators serve a six-year term—four years longer than that of any member of the House—and their election is staggered so that only one-third of the seats are contested at one time. Senatorial elections were designed this way so that members could presumably focus more on serving the nation than worrying about re-election. Elections were initially open only to the state legislatures, but after years of indecisive legislators and corrupt elections, the Seventeenth Amendment was passed in 1913 to establish popular election of senators.

> **When do senatorial elections take place and who votes in them?**
>
> _____
>
> _____

## SENATE LEADERSHIP

The Senate has its own leaders, although they are typically less powerful than those in the House. The Constitution mandates that the vice president of the United States act as the **president of the Senate**. Mostly a ceremonial position, the president of the Senate may preside over debates and break ties, although neither event happens very often.

The Constitution also directs the Senate to choose a **president pro tempore**, the person who presides in the absence of the president of the Senate and who is third in the line of succession for the presidency. Traditionally, this person is the senator from the majority party who has served the longest.

As in the House, the Senate elects party leaders and whips. The **Senate majority leader** is the most powerful person in the Senate, chosen by the majority

> **What is the most powerful position in the Senate?**
>
> _____

party during its caucus. As the party's Senate spokesperson and chief strategist, the Senate majority leader helps fellow party members with committee assignments and other issues—in return for their cooperation and support on legislation.

## COMMITTEES IN THE SENATE

Much of the work of senators is done in committee. The Senate has 16 standing committees—which include many subcommittees—and several select and special committees, whose job it is to examine a specific issue, advise the Senate as a whole, or provide oversight of government agencies. Senators also participate in joint and conference committees.

Senators are typically limited to sitting on no more than three committees and five subcommittees. The number of seats each party has on a committee reflects its numbers in the Senate, and assignments are made at the beginning of a congressional session, in a party conference or caucus. For the most part, priority is given according to seniority. The tradition of **seniority rule** also dictates that the most senior senator on a committee become chair. In the past, there have sometimes been term limits on chairs.

> **Explain seniority rule.**
> _____
> _____
> _____

Some committees have roles related to powers specific to the Senate. For example, the Judiciary Committee conducts hearings on nominees for federal judges before the Senate votes to confirm. Likewise, the Foreign Relations Committee has great influence on the Senate's role in ratifying treaties.

## RULES AND TRADITIONS

The Senate has several rules and tradition. It can expel or censure its members, although both practices are rare. Another rule involves filling vacancies, as directed by the Seventeenth Amendment: When a member dies or retires while in office, his or her state's governor appoints a replacement until a special election can be held. Perhaps the most well-known tradition is the **filibuster**, a Senate practice during which opponents of a measure take the floor and refuse to stop talking to prevent a vote from occurring. Only a two-thirds vote for **cloture**—an end to debate—can stop a filibuster.

> **What is the purpose of a filibuster?**
> _____

## Congress: The Legislative Branch

**Section 5**

**MAIN IDEA**
The main job of Congress is to make laws. The process of making laws is well established and orderly.

# Key Terms

**rider** a provision attached to a bill that bears little relationship to the bill's main topic

**joint resolution** Congressional action used in certain unusual circumstances that follows the same procedures as a bill and has the force of law if passed by both houses and signed by the president

**concurrent resolutions** Congressional actions without the force of law that are passed by both houses to address matters that affect the operations of both chambers

**discharge petition** a document that a majority of House members sign to force a bill out of committee

**Committee of the Whole** when all House members become members of a single committee to allow the House to function when many members are at hearings or are otherwise absent

**quorum** the number needed to legally conduct business

**roll-call vote** a vote in which each member is required to publicly state his or her vote, also known as a record vote

**conference committee** a committee formed when the House and Senate must reconcile different versions of the same bill

**pocket veto** an indirect veto that takes place when the president does not sign a bill within 10 days, during which time Congress adjourns

# Taking Notes

As you read, take notes on the process of making law in Congress. Record your notes in the graphic organizer below.

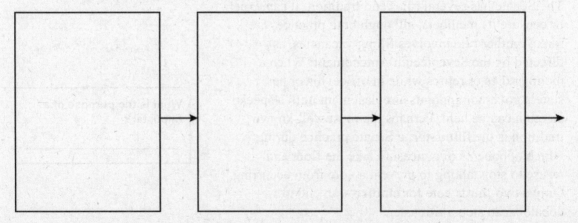

# Section Summary

## BILLS IN CONGRESS

Congress makes the nation's laws, which start out as bills. Only a member of Congress can submit a bill, but the idea behind a bill can come from Congress, constituents, interest groups, or the president. Private bills affect only a person or a small group; public bills affect all of society. Also, bills can involve a single subject or many. Many bills include **riders**, or attached provisions that have little to do with the rest of the bill but would otherwise be impossible to pass as legislation.

Besides bills, Congress also passes resolutions. **Joint resolutions** follow the same process as and sometimes have the same force as a bill, unlike other resolutions; they are used in specific, unusual situations. Both chambers pass **concurrent resolutions** when they need to address operations in both the House and Senate. Each chamber can also pass simple resolutions for its own individual operational issues. Finally, nonbinding resolutions give Congress an opportunity to express its opinion on an issue without legal impact.

> **Why would a member of Congress add a rider to a bill?**
>
> _____
>
> _____

## BILLS IN COMMITTEE

Most work on bills happens in committee. First, a bill is referred, either by the Speaker of the House or the Senate majority leader, to one or more committees, and then to a subcommittee. Next, the committee holds hearings, at which witnesses make statements on the bill. The subcommittee then votes to report a bill favorably, unfavorably, or no comment, and recommends whether the larger committee should take further action. In the House, subcommittees may amend a bill; in the Senate, the full committee amends bills.

> **How does a subcommittee learn more about a bill and its potential impact?**
>
> _____
>
> _____

After the subcommittee report, the full committee holds a meeting called a markup to discuss the report, examine the bill closely, and decide whether to report the bill as favorable, unfavorable, or without recommendation to the entire chamber. The committee can alternatively decide to take no further action, although in the House a majority of members can sign a **discharge petition** to force the bill out of committee. Another House-specific step in the process involves the powerful Rules Committee, which almost always assigns rules for amending the bill and time limits on debate.

## THE BILL ON THE FLOOR

Once a bill leaves committee in the House of Representatives, it is assigned rules by the Rules Committee, upon which the entire House votes. The Constitution dictates that the House can only conduct business when half its members are present—a number known as the **quorum**, currently at 218 members. When many members are at hearings or absent, the remaining members can form a **Committee of the Whole** and become members of one committee whose quorum is only 100. The committee then debates the bill and amends it as necessary, submitting its changes for a full House vote. Very important votes often require record votes, or **roll-call votes**, in which each member is required to publicly state his or her vote.

In the Senate, there is no Rules Committee, although a senator can request limits on a bill. These requests require a unanimous vote, which sometimes inspires a filibuster. After debating the bill, senators vote on the bill and any amendments, often by roll-call vote.

> **Why does the Senate sometimes need to form a Committee of the Whole?**
> _____
> _____

## THE CONFERENCE COMMITTEE

If majorly different versions of a bill pass in the House and Senate, a **conference committee** is formed to reconcile the differences. Once committee members from both chambers reach an agreement on a final bill, they issue a conference report. Both chambers must then vote to accept the report before the bill is sent to the president.

> **Why are conference committees formed?**
> _____

## PRESIDENTIAL ACTION ON A BILL

Once the president receives a bill, he or she can sign it, thereby making it law, or veto it. The president can also choose not to sign the bill, in which case it either becomes law after 10 days or is considered the victim of a **pocket veto** if Congress adjourns during that 10-day period.

# Chapter Summary

| The President | |
|---|---|
| Roles | chief executive, chief administrator, commander in chief, foreign policy leader, chief agenda setter, and unofficial roles |
| Qualifications | at least 35 years old, have lived in country at least 14 years, natural-born citizen, and unofficial qualifications |
| Powers | executive, diplomatic, military, judicial, and legislative powers |
| Administration | Executive Office of the President, vice president, cabinet |

## COMPREHENSION AND CRITICAL THINKING

Use information from the graphic organizer to answer the following questions.

1. **Identify** What types of powers do presidents have today?

_____

2. **Explain** Does it surprise you that the president has both official and unofficial roles?

_____

_____

3. **Develop** The vice president's and the cabinet's powers have expanded as the role of the president has increased over time. Why does this make sense?

_____

_____

Name _____ Class _____ Date _____

## The Presidency

**MAIN IDEA**
The Constitution gives only a brief description of the president's qualifications and powers. Yet the job is vast and complex, as the president must fulfill many roles.

# Key Terms and People

**chief executive** the role the president plays when executing, or carrying out, the nation's laws

**commander in chief** the role the president plays when ordering troops into action and calling them back home

**foreign policy** a nation's plans and procedures for dealing with other countries

**diplomacy** the art of negotiating with foreign governments

**chief of state** the role the president plays when acting as the symbolic figurehead of the United States

**succession** the process of succeeding, or coming after someone

# Taking Notes

As you read, take notes on the duties and qualifications of the president.
Record your notes in the graphic organizer below.

| The President | |
|---|---|
| Formal | Informal |
| | |

# Section Summary

## ROLES OF THE PRESIDENT

Article II of the Constitution outlines five official roles for the president. First, the president is **chief executive**, meaning he or she has the power to execute, or carry out, the nation's laws, both by running government programs and implementing laws passed by Congress. Next, the president is chief administrator, managing the executive departments that advise him or her. Third, the president acts as **commander in chief** of the military, holding the power to send troops into action and call them back home. Fourth, the president is the country's foreign policy leader. In this role, the president negotiates treaties, receives foreign ambassadors, and directs all efforts toward **diplomacy**—the art of negotiating with foreign governments. Through each of these activities, the president shapes the country's **foreign policy**, the United States' plans and procedures for dealing with other countries. Finally, the president acts as chief agenda setter when giving the annual State of the Union address and helping Congress with the budget.

Unofficially, the president is the **chief of state** when playing the role of symbolic figurehead of the United States. Although not stated in the Constitution, the president is also considered the head of his or her political party and, along with the vice president, the chief citizen—a representative of all American people.

> **Name the president's five official roles.**
>
> _____
>
> _____
>
> _____

## FORMAL CHARACTERISTICS OF THE PRESIDENCY

Article II of the Constitution also briefly outlines qualifications, terms of office, election, succession, and benefits. There are three formal qualifications. The president must be at least 35 years old, have lived in the country for 14 years, and be a natural-born citizen, meaning he or she was born a U.S. citizen. In recent years, this third qualification has come under much scrutiny, with critics claiming that it may block qualified candidates.

As for terms of office, the Constitution originally only stated that the president would serve a four-year term with the opportunity for re-election. After first president George Washington chose to serve two

> **Could a 45-year old woman who was born a French citizen become president? Explain.**
>
> _____
>
> _____
>
> _____

terms, a pattern was established and no president
served more than two terms until the 1940s, when
Franklin D. Roosevelt was elected to a third and then
a fourth term. Partially in response to this break in
tradition, the Twenty-second Amendment was added
to the Constitution in 1951, limiting the president to
two full terms and no more than 10 years in office.

As described in Chapter 3, the president and vice-
president are chosen by the electoral college. The
Constitution gives states the power to decide how to
pick these electors. The electoral college remains the
focus of much criticism, since states only receive the
same number of electors as it has members of
Congress. Therefore, small states receive
disproportionate representation in the election process.

Article II is unclear as to who formally succeeds the
president. For years, it was assumed that the vice
president would be next in the line of **succession**, the
process of succeeding or coming after someone. This
tradition became law when the Twenty-fifth
Amendment was passed in 1967. The Presidential
Succession Act of 1947 further extended the line of
succession, naming the Speaker of the House next in
line after the vice president.

> **Why were the Twenty-fifth Amendment and the Presidential Succession Act necessary?**
> _____
> _____
> _____
> _____

The Constitution also prevents Congress from
changing a president's salary while he or she is in
office. The president also has a personal staff, access
to air and ground transportation, health and retirement
benefits, tax deductions, and permission to live in the
White House for the duration of his or her term.

## INFORMAL QUALIFICATIONS FOR THE PRESIDENCY

Some qualifications for the presidency are not listed
within the Constitution but still play a major role in the
selection of the president. Although people of both
genders and many different ethnic and religious
backgrounds have run for president, with the exception
of Barack Obama, who made history as the first
African American president, every president as been a
white, well-educated male belonging to a Christian
denomination. Most have had some military
experience. Personality traits, like dignity, confidence,
and poise are also important to voters.

> **What have most past presidents had in common?**
> _____
> _____

Name _____ Class _____ Date _____

## The Presidency

**MAIN IDEA**
The powers of the presidency, outlined in Article II of the Constitution, are vast and have grown throughout the history of the United States. They are, however, checked by the other branches of government.

# Key Terms and People

**executive orders**  a formal rule or regulation instructing executive branch officials on how to carry out their jobs

**executive privilege**  the power of the president to refuse to release information to Congress or a court

**diplomatic recognition**  the president's power to formally recognize the legitimacy of a foreign government

**reprieve**  an act of clemency that postpones the carrying out of a sentence

**pardon**  an act of clemency that releases a convicted criminal from having to fulfill a sentence

**amnesty**  an act of clemency that grants a group of offenders a general pardon for offenses committed

**commute**  the president's power to reduce a person's sentence

# Taking Notes

As you read, take notes on the powers of the presidency. Record your notes in the graphic organizer below.

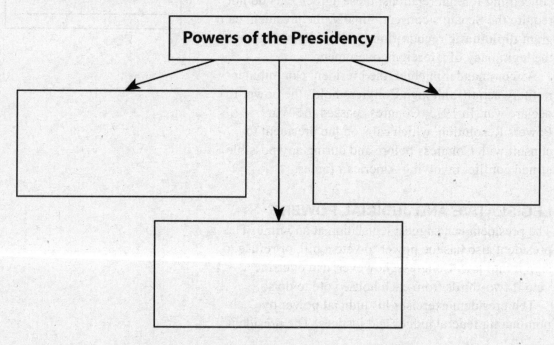

# Section Summary

## EXECUTIVE POWERS

The Constitution gives the president specific powers. First, the president directly appoints about 3,000 positions in the executive branch, a third of which need to be confirmed by the Senate. The president can use this power however he or she sees fit. With some exceptions, the president can remove appointees at any time.

Through interpretation of Article II, Section 3 of the Constitution, presidents also have the power to issue **executive orders**, formal, signed statements that instruct or guide executive officials and have the force of law. These are different than signing statements, which make modifications to existing laws. Constitutional interpretation also grants the president the right of **executive privilege**, which allows a president to refuse to release information to Congress or a court.

## DIPLOMATIC AND MILITARY POWERS

As foreign policy leader, the president can negotiate treaties, although the Senate needs to approve and can override them. Presidents can also make executive agreements with the heads of other countries concerning foreign relations; these agreements do not require the Senate's consent. Finally, the president can grant **diplomatic recognition** by formally recognizing the legitimacy of a foreign government.

As commander in chief, the president can initiate military action, although Congress holds the power to declare war. In 1973, Congress passed the War Powers Resolution, which calls on the president to consult with Congress before and during any possible armed conflict involving American forces.

> What is one way that treaties and executive agreements differ?
>
> _____
>
> _____

## LEGISLATIVE AND JUDICIAL POWERS

The president can suggest legislation at any time. The president also has the power to veto a bill, or refuse to sign it into law. Congress, however, can override a veto if two-thirds from each house vote to do so.

The president exercises his judicial power by nominating federal judges and justices. The president can also give **reprieves**, which postpone jail time, or **pardons**, which release a convicted criminal from a sentence; offer **amnesty**, which grants a group of offenders a general pardon; and **commute**, or reduce, sentences. These four powers of clemency, or mercy, only apply to federal cases and cannot be used in impeachment cases.

> **What are the president's four powers of clemency?**
>
> _____
>
> _____
>
> _____
>
> _____

## INFORMAL POWERS

The president's informal powers stem from access to the media and his or her position as party leader. With constant media coverage, the president can reach out to the public for support at any time. As party leader, the president typically has the support of fellow party members in Congress.

## CHECKS ON THE PRESIDENT'S POWERS

The president's powers can be formally checked by judicial review, blocked nominations, and veto overrides. The media and public approval are sources of informal checks on the president's power.

## CHANGES IN PRESIDENTIAL POWER

Until the late nineteenth century, the executive branch played a much less powerful role than the legislative branch. However, as the United States entered world wars and became a major player in international politics, Americans began to expect more of the men representing it. Presidents like Lyndon B. Johnson initiated social problems that strengthened the connection between presidents and the people. As mass media further developed, from print to radio to television to the Internet, presidents found an expanded outlet for reaching out to the public for support. Today's presidents maintain this relationship by fully taking advantage of the exposure the media gives them, ensuring that they and their policies remain prominent in the public eye.

> **How can a president use the media to his or her advantage?**
>
> _____
>
> _____

**The Presidency**

**MAIN IDEA**
The president leads a large team of people who help carry out the duties of the office. This team includes a staff of advisers, the vice president, and members of the cabinet.

# Key Terms

**administration**  the group of people who work for the executive branch under a specific president

**Executive Office of the President**  the organizational structure that helps manages the executive programs and agencies

**White House Office**  a central office of the Executive Office of the President in which many key assistants and deputy assistants to the president work

**chief of staff**  the person who manages the White House Office

**National Security Council**  an executive office that brings together the top military, foreign affairs, and intelligence officials to coordinate U.S. national security

**Council of Economic Advisers**  an executive office that provides the president with expert analysis of the economy

**Office of Management and Budget**  an executive office that helps develop and implement the federal budget and to oversee its execution by the agencies in the executive branch

**executive departments**  departments within the president's administration that are responsible for carrying out laws, administering programs, and making regulations in their particular area of responsibility

# Taking Notes

As you read, take notes on the president's administration. Record your notes in the graphic organizer below.

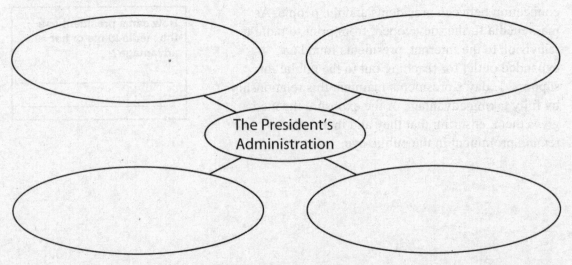

# Section Summary

## EXECUTIVE OFFICE OF THE PRESIDENT

The group of people who work for the executive branch under a president are known as the president's **administration**. Up until the twentieth century, presidents had a relatively small number of staff. Beginning with Theodore Roosevelt, the number of executive programs and agencies began to increase, making it necessary to better manage these many offices. In 1939 Congress authorized the creation of the **Executive Office of the President** (EOP), an organizational structure under which the president's many advisers and assistants fall. Almost all members are appointed by the president and confirmed by the Senate.

Several important offices fall under the EOP. The **White House Office** includes many key assistants and advisers to the president. Within this office is the president's **chief of staff**. This position consists of different responsibilities depending on the president in office, but can include managing everyday office operations, mapping political strategy, and handling relations with Congress and the cabinet. The chief of staff also manages the people responsible for delivering the president's message, including speechwriters and the White House press secretary.

Formed during the Cold War to combat the influence of the nation's enemies, the **National Security Council** (NSC) is chaired by the president, with the presidentially-appointed national security adviser working as his or her second in command. The Council meets regularly to coordinate issues of U.S. national security. These meetings are also attended by the vice president, several cabinet members, and the chairman of the Joint Chiefs of Staff, a group made up of the heads of each major branch of the armed forces.

The **Council of Economic Advisers** (CEA) has been part of the EOP since 1946. This office consists of three nominated and confirmed members, as well as a staff of assistants and advisers. The CEA advises the president on his or her economic policy and U.S. economic performance. Members also help the president prepare the detailed annual *Economic Report*.

> Why was the Executive Office of the President created?
>
> _____
>
> _____

> What is the purpose of the National Security Council?
>
> _____
>
> _____
>
> _____

The **Office of Management and Budget** (OMB) is the largest office within the EOP, headed by a nominated and confirmed director. Its purpose is to help develop and implement the federal budget, legislation, and government regulations, as well as set policies on government finance and purchases. Members work with both the executive and legislative branches.

## THE VICE PRESIDENT

The vice presidency is the only administrative office besides the president that is an elected position. The vice president is assigned three responsibilities by the Constitution: preside over the Senate, open and count the electoral votes in a presidential election, and serve as president if the president is unable. Until recently, most vice presidents did very little else, with the exception of helping to get the president elected or re-elected. Starting in the 1970s, presidents began to rely more heavily on their vice presidents for advice and to manage certain executive projects.

> How has the role of the vice president changed in recent decades?
>
> _____
> _____
> _____

## THE CABINET

The cabinet is an organization made up of the heads, or secretaries, of the **executive departments**. These departments carry out laws, administer programs, and create regulations in their area of responsibility. Each secretary is nominated by the president and confirmed by the Senate. Secretaries both advise the president and run their own department. There are 16 official cabinet positions, including the vice president. Presidents can also invite other people to sit on the cabinet if necessary.

The power to create and expand the cabinet comes from an interpretation of the Constitution, which says that the president "may require the opinion, in writing, of the principal officer of each of the executive departments." The experience and background of cabinet members vary from president to president, as does the degree to which the president depends upon members' advice.

> Where does the president's power to create a cabinet come from?
>
> _____
> _____

# The Executive Branch at Work

## Chapter Summary

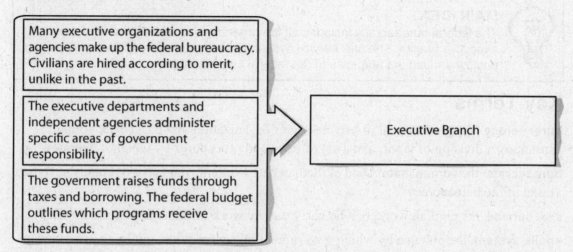

Many executive organizations and agencies make up the federal bureaucracy. Civilians are hired according to merit, unlike in the past.

The executive departments and independent agencies administer specific areas of government responsibility.

The government raises funds through taxes and borrowing. The federal budget outlines which programs receive these funds.

Executive Branch

## COMPREHENSION AND CRITICAL THINKING

Use information from the graphic organizer to answer the following questions.

1. **Recall**  What is the role of the executive departments and independent agencies?

   _____

   _____

2. **Summarize**  How does the government raise funds?

   _____

   _____

3. **Draw Conclusions**  Why is the executive branch divided into so many smaller agencies?

   _____

   _____

## The Executive Branch at Work

**Section 1**

**MAIN IDEA**
The federal bureaucracy includes all the organizations and agencies of the executive branch. The civil service system is used to place qualified civilians into positions within the agencies of the federal bureaucracy.

# Key Terms

**bureaucracy** any government or private-sector organization that has a clear formal structure, a division of labor, and a set of rules and procedures by which it operates

**bureaucrats** the administrators and skilled, expert workers who carry out many specific tasks of the bureaucracy

**civil service** the civilian workers who carry out the work of the federal government

**spoils system** the practice by which government jobs were given out by the president as political rewards to people who supported that president's policies or election campaign

# Taking Notes

As you read, take notes on what makes up the federal bureaucracy. Record your notes in the graphic organizer below.

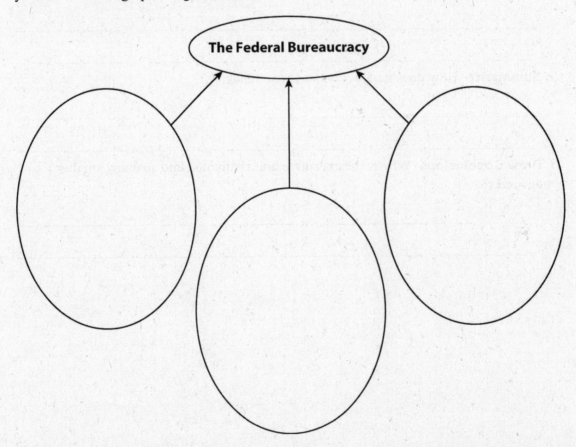

The Federal Bureaucracy

# Section Summary

## WHAT IS THE FEDERAL BUREAUCRACY?

A **bureaucracy** is a government or private-sector organization that has a clear, formal structure; a division of labor; and a set of rules and procedures by which it operates. The federal bureaucracy is the overarching organization that includes all of the executive branch's agencies and departments. Contained within the federal bureaucracy are the office of the vice president and the Executive Office of the President, the executive departments, and the three types of independent agencies: independent executive agencies, independent regulatory commissions, and government corporations.

There are currently about 2.7 million people working within the federal bureaucracy. The top administrators are either appointed by the president or nominated by the president and then approved by the Senate. These political appointees usually leave when a president's term of office is complete. However, **bureaucrats**, or the administrators and skilled workers who carry out many specific tasks of the federal bureaucracy, typically keep their jobs regardless of who is in office. Bureaucrats get their jobs through a competitive hiring process and are experts who help the bureaucracy implement legislation and executive orders.

| What is a bureaucracy? |
| :--- |
| _____ |
| _____ |
| _____ |

## THE CIVIL SERVICE

The **civil service** is the name given to the group of civilians who carry out the work of the federal government. Any nonmilitary government worker is considered a member of the civil service. The people who work in the civil service are hired through a competitive selection process.

Job placement within the civil service did not always follow this competitive process. Up until the late 1800s, the president usually gave out government jobs as rewards to people who supported his campaign or the president's policies while in office—a practice called the **spoils system**. Many Americans grew tired of the spoils system by the late 1800s, criticizing the government corruption, with political appointees rewarding supporters with contracts for work on

| Describe the spoils system. |
| :--- |
| _____ |
| _____ |
| _____ |

federal projects. In addition, each time a new
president came to office, existing workers were fired
and new employees hired. Most workers had little
time to build skills, making the federal bureaucracy
inconsistent and difficult to stabilize.

Early attempts to reform the civil-service system
were largely unsuccessful. The Civil Service
Commission, created by Congress in 1871, had too
little funding to change hiring and placement
practices. However, after the assassination of
President James Garfield by a disappointed office
seeker, the legislative and executive branches began to
take more action. In 1883 the Pendleton Civil Service
Act became law. The act directed all hiring and
promotions to be based on merit, not party affiliation.
The Pendleton Act also created a new Civil Service
Commission, whose job it was to administer objective
exams to potential employees and hire only those
whose test scores proved them to be qualified.

Today, the reach of the Pendleton Civil Service Act
encompasses even more workers, due partly to
additional legislation. The Civil Service Reform Act
of 1978 established new agencies whose job it is to
manage the civil service. The Office of Personnel
Management runs the civil-service system, testing and
placing job applicants, and manages the administrative
functions of the civil service. The Federal Labor
Relations Authority handles and attempts to resolve
complaints about unfair labor practices. The United
States Merit Systems Protection Board protects civil-
service employees from politically-motivated hiring
practices and other abuses. More than 90 percent of
government jobs are now protected by civil-service
legislation.

> **How did the Pendleton Act prevent the spoils system from returning?**
>
> _____
>
> _____
>
> _____

**The Executive Branch at Work**

**MAIN IDEA**
Executive departments and independent agencies provide key services and regulate important industries for the American people.

## Key Terms

**independent agencies** government agencies that operate separately from the executive departments

**independent executive agencies** independent agencies whose purpose is to oversee and manage a specific aspect of the federal government

**independent regulatory commissions** independent agencies whose purpose is to regulate some aspect of the economy

**bipartisan** including members from both major political parties

**government corporations** independent agencies that are organized and run like businesses but are owned in whole or in part by the federal government

## Taking Notes

As you read, take notes on the executive departments and independent agencies. Record your notes in the graphic organizer below.

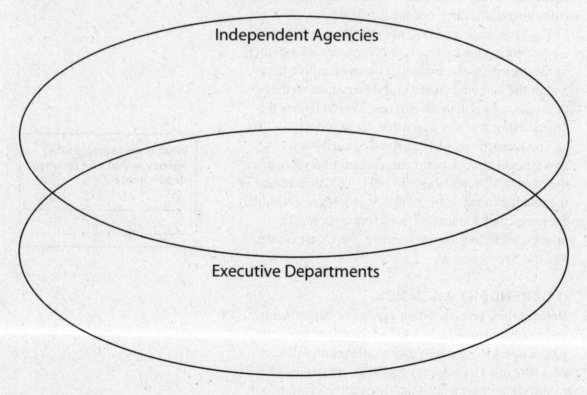

# Section Summary

## EXECUTIVE DEPARTMENTS

The 15 executive departments, which are headed by members of the cabinet, employ about 60 percent of all federal government employees. They are the primary units of both administration and policy-making in the executive branch. Every department focuses on its own general area of responsibility, and smaller agencies within each department focus on more specific issues. While the president has the power to nominate high-level positions in these departments, the Senate must confirm these nominations. Congress also controls the departments' duties, powers, and budgets.

> **How is Congress involved with the executive departments?**
> _____
> _____
> _____

## THE DEPARTMENTS TODAY

Today, there are 15 executive departments. Each has important goals and functions.

The goal of the Department of Health and Human Services (HHS) is to protect Americans' health. It administers Social Security, Medicare, and Medicaid. Agencies within HHS, such as the Food and Drug Administration, carry out specific tasks.

The Department of Defense (DOD) is responsible for protecting the nation. It encompasses all members of the armed forces, including those on active duty and in the National Guard and Reserve, as well as thousands of civilian employees. The DOD has the largest budget of any executive department.

The Department of Homeland Security is the newest executive department, created two years after the attacks of September 11, 2001. This department is the result of a reorganization of agencies responsible for protecting Americans from further domestic attacks, including border security, the Coast Guard, and the Secret Service.

> **What is an example of an agency within an executive department?**
> _____
> _____

## INDEPENDENT AGENCIES

Besides the agencies within executive departments, there are approximately 140 **independent agencies**, which operate separately from the executive departments. Each agency has been created by Congress to meet a need that legislation cannot, and ultimately remains under the control of Congress.

**Independent executive agencies** oversee and manage a specific aspect of the federal government. Similar in power and sometimes in organization to executive departments, these agencies often fulfill a president's strategic vision, as the Peace Corps did for President John F. Kennedy. The National Aeronautics and Space Administration (NASA) is another example of an independent executive agency.

**Independent regulatory commissions** regulate some aspect of the economy. They are run by three- to seven-person boards whose members are nominated by the president and confirmed by the Senate. Boards must be **bipartisan**, or include members from both major political parties. The commissions can create, implement, and enforce its own laws, although Congress can override them if necessary.

**Government corporations** are the third type of independent agency, organized and run like businesses but partially or fully owned by the federal government. They are created when the government recognizes that a private corporation cannot meet a specific national need for a sufficient profit. The U.S. Postal Service and AMTRAK are both government corporations that were established when Congress realized that geography was preventing private mail and rail companies from offering affordable service to all Americans.

> **How does Congress decide when to create a government corporation?**
> _____
> _____
> _____
> _____

## POWER AND ACCOUNTABILITY IN THE FEDERAL BUREAUCRACY

The Constitution provides tools for ensuring the accountability of the federal bureaucracy. The president and Congress both exercise checks on the federal bureaucracy. Over the years, Congress has passed legislation to check agencies, including setting guidelines for agency rules and making information available to the public. However, sometimes agencies, congressional committees, and interest groups form alliances in which each group benefits from the actions of the others. These relationships are labeled *iron triangles* because outsiders, including the president, cannot seem to penetrate it.

> **How has Congress checked the power of the independent agencies?**
> _____
> _____

## The Executive Branch at Work

**MAIN IDEA**
By collecting taxes and borrowing money, the federal government is able to generate the funds it needs to run the nation. The government then assigns these funds to create a federal budget for the upcoming year.

# Key Terms

**income tax** a tax on a person's or corporation's income

**progressive tax** a tax whose rates increase as the amount subject to taxation increases

**payroll tax** a tax that is withheld from a person's paycheck by his or her employer to help pay for forms of social insurance

**regressive tax** a tax that has a greater impact on lower-income earners than on upper-income earners

**proportional tax** a tax that is applied at the same rate against all income

**bond** a financial instrument by which a borrower agrees to pay back borrowed money, plus interest, at a future date

**federal debt** the total amount of money that the government has borrowed and not repaid

**mandatory spending** a type of government spending that is mandated by federal laws and is not subject to the annual budget process

**discretionary spending** a type of government spending that is subject to the annual budget process

**fiscal policy** a financial policy that involves creating the federal budget and taxation laws

**monetary policy** a financial policy that involves altering the amount of money in circulation and the interest rates at which money is borrowed

# Taking Notes

As you read, take notes on financing the federal government. Record your notes in a graphic organizer like the one below.

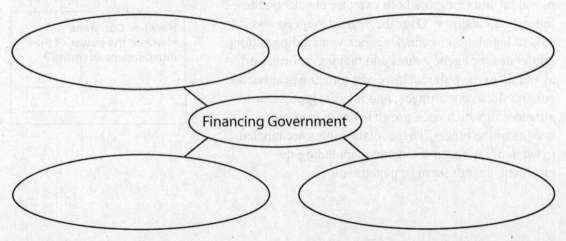

# Section Summary

## PAYING FOR GOVERNMENT

The federal government pays for its programs and services by collecting revenue and by borrowing.

The largest percentage of the federal government's revenue—around 61 percent—comes from **income taxes**, which are taxes on a person's or corporation's income. The income tax is an example of a **progressive tax**—a tax whose rates increase as the amount that is subject to taxation increases. **Payroll taxes**, money withheld from a person's paycheck that helps pay for Social Security, Medicare, and other forms of social insurance, are examples of a **regressive tax**. This kind of tax only applies to income up to a certain amount and therefore impacts lower-income earners more than upper-income earners. The Social Security tax is a regressive tax. The Medicare tax is both a regressive and a **proportional tax**, a tax that is applied at the same rate against all income.

> **Why is a proportional tax also a regressive tax?**
> _____
> _____
> _____
> _____

The government collects a much smaller amount of its revenue—about six percent—from excise taxes; tariffs, or taxes on imported goods; estate taxes, or taxes on money and property passed on to heirs when someone dies; gift taxes, or taxes on money or property given to one living person from another; and non-tax sources, such as entrance fees to national parks.

Additionally, the government borrows money by selling **bonds**, financial instruments by which the government agrees to pay back the borrowed money, plus interest, at a future date. In the past, the government only sold bonds in emergencies. However, in recent decades, economic depressions have led to almost continuous budget deficits, which occur when a government's revenues are lower than its expenses. Bond sales have therefore increased. The total amount of borrowed money yet to be repaid is called the **federal debt**. As long as the government is operating under a deficit, it will pay only the interest on the debt.

> **How does the government borrow money?**
> _____
> _____

## GOVERNMENT SPENDING

There are two types of government spending.
**Mandatory spending** is spending mandated by laws
and not subject to the annual budget process.
**Discretionary spending** is spending that is subject to
the annual budget process. The president and
Congress most work together closely to decide how
and where to use these discretionary funds.

## THE BUDGET PROCESS

The federal budget is first prepared by the president,
who is assisted by the Office of Management and
Budget. The president presents the budget to Congress
by the first Monday in February. Next, Congress and
the nonpartisan Congressional Budget Office review
and modify the budget. Then the House and Senate
Budget Committees hold hearings on and eventually
pass a concurrent resolution that includes the year's
grand totals for revenue and spending. Once the
resolution is in place, the House and Senate
Appropriations Committees assign discretionary
funding to programs and write appropriations bills
that reflect these spending decisions. The bills are then
sent to the president to sign, ideally by October 1, the
beginning of the government's fiscal year.

> **Who decides which programs will receive discretionary funding?**
> _____
> _____

## FISCAL AND MONETARY POLICY

Government spending and borrowing affects the
economy enormously. When they create the budget
and tax laws, the president and Congress are making a
**fiscal policy**. This kind of policy can be used to
stimulate the economy by spending money in specific
areas or by cutting taxes. When the government
changes the amount of money in circulation or interest
rates, it is creating a **monetary policy**. An
independent regulatory commission called the Federal
Reserve System, or the Fed, actually controls
monetary policy. It does this by raising or lowering
the amount of money banks must have in reserve,
raising or lowering the interest rate it charges banks,
and buying or selling bonds. The government uses
both fiscal and monetary policy to work toward
economic growth, low unemployment, stable prices
for goods and services, and a balanced budget.

> **How does fiscal policy stimulate the economy?**
> _____
> _____
> _____

## The Federal Courts and the Judicial Branch

# Chapter Summary

| The Federal Court System |
| :--- |
| The Constitution created a three-level court system, with district courts on the bottom and the Supreme Court on top. |

| District Courts | Courts of Appeals | Supreme Court |
| :--- | :--- | :--- |
| Trial courts, with original jurisdiction for most federal cases | Appellate courts hear cases appealed from district courts and some federal agencies | Highest court in the nation, ruling on questions of federal law and the Constitution |

## COMPREHENSION AND CRITICAL THINKING

Use information from the graphic organizer to answer the following questions.

1. **Describe** What is the structure of the U.S. federal court system?

_____

_____

2. **Explain** Why do you think the courts of appeals are higher than the district courts?

_____

_____

3. **Predict** The Supreme Court's power has increased over time as the nation has turned to the Court to decide questions of federal and constitutional law. Do you think the Court's importance will continue to increase or will it decrease? Explain.

_____

_____

# The Federal Courts and the Judicial Branch

**MAIN IDEA**
The Framers created an independent judicial branch as part of the separation of powers of the national government. At the federal level, the judicial branch consists of three tiers of courts, each performing a different function.

## Key Terms

**jurisdiction** the authority to hear and decide a case

**exclusive jurisdiction** the sole right to hear a case

**concurrent jurisdiction** when both state courts and federal courts have the right to hear a case

**plaintiff** the person making a legal complaint

**defendant** the person against whom a legal complaint is filed

**original jurisdiction** a court's right to have heard a case simply because it was the first court to hear it

**appellate jurisdiction** a court's right to hear a case once it has been appealed from a lower court

**judicial restraint** the concept that a judge should interpret the Constitution according to the Framers' original intention

**judicial activism** the concept that judges can adapt the meaning of the Constitution to contemporary realities

**precedent** previous court rulings on a given legal question

**senatorial courtesy** tradition in which a senator from the same state as a judicial nominee and from the same political party as the president can block the nominee and expect no opposition from other senators

## Taking Notes

As you read, take notes on the federal court system. Record your notes in the graphic organizer below.

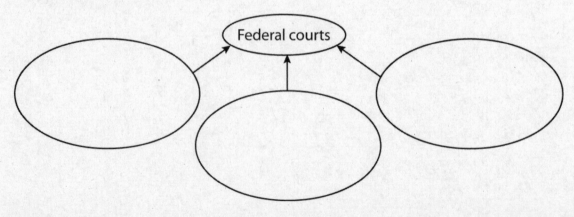

Federal courts

# Section Summary

## THE AMERICAN COURT SYSTEM

Courts perform three functions: they identify if a law has been broken and if penalties apply, they decide how to provide relief to those who have been harmed, and, if relevant, they determine the meaning of a specific law or part of the Constitution.

When the Framers wrote the Constitution, they chose to keep the existing state courts and add a federal court system. They created specific rules for **jurisdiction**, or the authority to hear and decide a case. Today, state courts, directed by state laws and constitutions, hear the majority of cases. Federal courts have **exclusive jurisdiction**, or the sole right to hear a case, in certain situations, such as when a case involves the interpretation of the Constitution or a foreign ambassador.

In some cases, courts have **concurrent jurisdiction** and the **plaintiff**, or person making the legal complaint, can file the case in either state or federal court. However, the **defendant**, or person against whom the complaint is filed, can sometimes insist that the case is heard in federal court.

The court that first hears a case is said to have **original jurisdiction**. Any court that hears the case at a higher level is said to have **appellate jurisdiction**.

| What three purposes do courts fulfill? |
| --- |
| _____ |
| _____ |
| _____ |
| _____ |
| _____ |

## STRUCTURE OF THE FEDERAL COURT SYSTEM

Since the Constitution is vague about how the federal court system should be structured, Congress has passed laws to determine the types and purposes of federal courts. The Judiciary Act of 1789 set up a three-tiered federal court structure. The 94 district courts are on the lowest level. These trial courts have original jurisdiction over almost all federal criminal and civil cases. Courts of appeals make up the middle level of the federal court system. These 13 courts hear appeals from the lower courts and from certain federal agencies. Finally, the Supreme Court is the entire top tier of the system. Although the Court does have original jurisdiction in a few very special situations, it acts mainly as the ultimate appellate court in the United States. Each year, its chief justice and eight

| Summarize the three tiers of the federal court system, including each tier's jurisdiction. |
| --- |
| _____ |
| _____ |
| _____ |
| _____ |
| _____ |

associates review about 80 cases involving the Constitution or federal law.

Since the original Judiciary Act, Congress has added a number of other courts whose jurisdiction is limited to cases that Congress specifies. Judges in these special courts do not have guaranteed pay or lifetime appointment, as do all other federal judges.

## APPOINTING FEDERAL JUDGES

When nominating federal judges, presidents must consider four factors. First, the president must consider the person's legal expertise. Next, the president must consider the person's party affiliation; most presidents pick nominees from their own party.

Third, the president needs to think about whether the person's judicial philosophy and respect for **precedent**, or previous court rulings on a given legal question, matches his or her own. Presidents typically gauge judicial philosophy by identifying where the prospective nominee falls along the spectrum of **judicial restraint**—the concept that a judge should interpret the Constitution according to the Framers' original intention—and **judicial activism**—the concept that judges can adapt the meaning of the Constitution to contemporary realities.

Finally, the president must consider whether the Senate will approve the person. If a district court judge is nominated, a senator from the same state as the nominee and the same party as the president can block the nominee with little argument from other senators. This practice is called **senatorial courtesy**.

> Which end of the judicial spectrum would include a strict interpretation of the Constitution?
>
> _____
>
> _____

## CHECKS AND BALANCES

Under the system of checks and balances, the judicial branch checks the legislative and executive branches through the power of judicial review. In return, the other two branches check the judicial branch through the appointment process of judges, the amendment process, and with the power to impeach and remove judges. This last check is extremely difficult to exercise, since judicial independence, or the freedom to rule without fear of political retaliation, is carefully guarded by American society.

> Identify two ways that the other two branches can check the judicial branch.
>
> _____
>
> _____
>
> _____
>
> _____

# The Federal Courts and the Judicial Branch

**MAIN IDEA**
Congress has created a system of lower courts for the federal judicial system.
Each court has a specific role to play in the judicial branch.

## Key Terms

**grand juries** panels of citizens that hear evidence of a possible crime and recommend whether the evidence is sufficient to file criminal charges

**bankruptcy** a legal process by which citizens who cannot pay money they owe others can receive court protection and assistance in settling their financial problems

**magistrate judges** district-court officials who are appointed for eight years and hear some of the early hearings of criminal trials as well as some misdemeanor and civil cases

**misdemeanor** a minor criminal case punishable by one year or less of prison time

**public defenders** lawyers provided to defendants who cannot afford to hire a lawyer

**marshals** officials who provide security and police protection at federal courthouses

**appellant** a person who files an appeal to have their case reviewed by a court of appeals

**briefs** written arguments

**sovereign immunity** principle that a sovereign nation is immune from being sued unless it agrees to be sued

**courts-martial** hearings held by the U.S. Court of Appeals for the Armed Forces to decide cases involving violation of the Uniform Code of Military Justice

## Taking Notes

As you read, take notes on the federal court system. Record your notes in the graphic organizer below.

| District Courts | Courts of Appeals | Other Courts |
|---|---|---|
|  |  |  |

# Section Summary

## FEDERAL DISTRICT COURTS

The 94 district courts each have between two and 44 judges. These judges hear over 400,000 cases a year. These cases range those that are directly assigned to the federal courts by the Constitution to cases concerning a variety of criminal and civil offenses. Serious criminal cases involve a **grand jury**, a panel of 16 to 23 citizens who hear evidence of a crime and recommend whether the evidence is sufficient to file criminal charges.

Federal judges are nominated by the president, approved by the Senate, and have no set term. The exception to this involves bankruptcy judges, who serve 14-year terms and are appointed by the local circuit's Court of Appeals. These judges preside in bankruptcy court, a smaller part of a district court. They only hear cases involving **bankruptcy**, a legal process by which people who cannot pay money they owe others can receive court protection and assistance.

Judges play the most important role in a federal court, presiding over trials, ensuring proper legal procedures, and instructing juries. **Magistrate judges**, appointed by federal judges for eight-year terms, are responsible for overseeing parts of criminal trials and some civil cases and **misdemeanor** cases—minor criminal cases that have a maximum punishment of one year in prison. Each district court also has a clerk of the court, who performs administrative duties.

There are three other groups of officials who are heavily involved in the operations of a district court. The first group is the U.S. attorneys. U.S. attorneys are appointed by the president and represent the United States in federal court. For example, when a person is charged with a federal crime, the U.S. attorney acts as a prosecutor. The second group is the **public defenders**, lawyers assigned to defendants who cannot afford to hire one, are present in every federal court. The third and final group is the U.S. **marshals**, who provide security and police protection at federal courthouses. Marshals also track criminal suspects and protect witnesses.

> **What is the purpose of a grand jury?**
> _____
> _____
> _____

> **Explain the role of a U.S. attorney in a federal district court.**
> _____
> _____

## FEDERAL COURTS OF APPEALS

There is one court of appeals for each of the 12 U.S. regional circuits and an additional Court of Appeals for the Federal District, which only hears cases related to specific areas of the law. Each year, the 13 courts hear about 55,000 cases on appeal from district courts and certain federal agencies, but fewer than nine percent of appeals are successful. In order for an appellate court to overturn a previous ruling, the **appellant**, or person who filed the appeal, needs to show that the original ruling was affected by a legal mistake. During the appeal, a randomly chosen panel of three circuit judges examines the factual record from the first trial and reads **briefs**, or written arguments, from both sides. The panel then decides the case based on precedents from Supreme Court rulings and the circuit court's own earlier rulings.

Almost all rulings by a court of appeals are final. In rare situations, a case may be sent back to the district court for additional hearings, the original prosecutor may retry a case, or an *en banc* review may take place, during which other judges from the court examine the case. Additionally, a very small number of rulings are reviewed by the Supreme Court each year.

> **What does an appellant need to prove in order to have a successful appeal?**
> _____
> _____
> _____
> _____

## OTHER FEDERAL COURTS

Besides the district and appellate courts, Congress has created several special federal courts with very limited jurisdictions. These include courts just for Washington, D.C. and the U.S. territories, a court to hear cases involving international trade, a tax court for federal-tax cases, and a court of appeals to hear veterans' claims. The U.S. Court of Federal Claims hears complaints against the U.S. government in cases where **sovereign immunity**, or the nation's immunity from being sued unless agreeing to it, does not apply.

In addition, the Foreign Intelligence Surveillance Court, the Alien Terrorist Removal Court, and military commissions that try people captured by U.S. armed forces all hear cases involving national security. The U.S. Court of Appeals for the Armed Forces holds hearings called **courts-martial** to decide cases involving violation of military code.

> **Name three other federal courts created by Congress.**
> _____
> _____
> _____

# The Federal Courts and the Judicial Branch

**MAIN IDEA**
The Supreme Court is the highest court in the nation and the most important component of the judicial branch. It serves as the final word on questions of federal law and the Constitution.

## Key Terms

**writ of certiorari** an order issued by the Supreme Court to review a lower court's decision

**docket** the list of cases to be heard

**majority opinion** a court opinion signed by at least five of the nine justices of the Supreme Court

**concurring opinions** court opinions that agree with the overall conclusion in a case but stress different or additional legal reasoning

**dissenting opinions** court opinions held by the minority of justices who do not agree with the ruling in a case

## Taking Notes

As you read, take notes on the Supreme Court. Record your notes in the graphic organizer below.

| History | Appointments | Procedures |
|---------|--------------|------------|
|         |              |            |
|         |              |            |
|         |              |            |
|         |              |            |

# Section Summary

## HIGHLIGHTS OF SUPREME COURT HISTORY

The Supreme Court has experienced many shifts in political power since the Constitution was ratified. Alexander Hamilton was the first to really explain the Court's purpose and the importance of its judicial review of acts of Congress and the executive branch. But it was not until 1801, when John Marshall was appointed chief justice, that Court rulings began to have a major effect on Americans. Under Marshall, the judicial branch became an equal of the two other branches, issuing important rulings on the reach of judicial review, the implied powers of Congress, and interstate commerce.

In 1857 the Court's decision in *Dred Scott* v. *Sandford* threw the country into an uproar that eventually led to the Civil War. In their decision, the justices declared that a slave brought to a free territory was not actually free and could not become a citizen. Furthermore, the Court ruled that Congress did not have the power to outlaw slavery in territories.

In the years after the Civil War, the Court narrowly interpreted the Thirteenth, Fourteenth, and Fifteenth Amendments in relation to civil rights. The Court struck down the Civil Rights Act of 1875, stating that it was the responsibility of the states, not the federal government, to protect African Americans from discrimination.

Throughout the twentieth century, the Court has ruled in other landmark decisions. These decisions cover a wide-range of issues from economic regulation to desegregation to individuals' rights.

> **What did the *Dred Scott* decision demonstrate about the relationship between the Supreme Court and Congress?**
>
> _____
> _____
> _____

## CHOOSING SUPREME COURT JUSTICES

As they do with all other federal judicial nominees, presidents must consider each Supreme Court nominee's legal expertise, party affiliation, judicial philosophy, and acceptability to the Senate. Almost all justices have had a background in law, and most have belonged to the same party and shared the same beliefs about Constitutional interpretation as the nominating president. Typically, nominees are carefully evaluated to ensure that they will not inspire strong opposition within the Senate.

> **What do most Supreme Court nominees have in common?**
>
> _____
> _____
> _____
> _____

Conducted by the Senate Judiciary Committee, the hearings for a Supreme Court nominee are televised and usually intense. The nominee is questioned about past writings and decisions, judicial beliefs, and even his or her personal background. Senators often try to gauge the nominee's likeliness to judge one way or the other on a major issue, but their efforts are usually unsuccessful. When the hearings are complete, the committee votes on the nominee, after which the Senate votes as a whole. Senators not on the Senate Judiciary Committee almost always follow the lead of the committee's vote.

> **What information do members of the Senate Judiciary Committee seek during a Supreme Court nominee's hearings?**
>
> _____
> _____
> _____
> _____

## SUPREME COURT PROCEDURES

The Supreme Court is in session from early October to June or July, during which time the justices alternate between one week of hearing cases and one week of working on rulings and upcoming cases. There are three ways that a case can be placed on the Court's **docket**, or list of cases to be heard. First, the Court has original jurisdiction in select cases, such as those involving disputes between states. Second, the Court can issue a **writ of certiorari**, an order seeking review of a lower court's case. Third, a state case can arrive at the Court if it has already gone through appeals but still involves a question about the Constitution or federal law.

When the Supreme Court hears a case, it first reads briefs, or written arguments, submitted by each side and sometimes by outside parties. The Court then hears and questions 30 minutes of oral arguments from each side. Next, the justices study and discuss the case behind closed doors. They then issue their decision within an opinion, a detailed written explanation of the major issues, judicial precedents, and legal reasoning behind the decision. This entire process is called plenary review.

There is more than one type of court opinion. A **majority opinion** is signed by at least five of the nine justices and represents the actual ruling. **Concurring opinions** agree with the overall conclusion of the case but stress other legal reasoning as well. **Dissenting opinions** are issued by those justices who did not agree with the majority opinion.

> **When the Supreme Court issues a ruling, do all of the justices always agree? Explain.**
>
> _____
> _____
> _____

## The Political Process

# Chapter Summary

**COMPREHENSION AND CRITICAL THINKING**
Use information from the graphic organizer to answer the following
questions.

1. **Describe** What do interest groups do?

   _____

2. **Make Generalizations** Think of an important issue in American government today.
   How might public opinion influence how lawmakers address the issue?

   _____

   _____

3. **Declare** Voting behavior is mainly affected by party identification, personal views, a
   candidate's background, and the voter's background. How do you think political
   parties target these factors?

   _____

   _____

## The Political Process

**MAIN IDEA**
Public opinion is the collection of views that people hold on public issues. Public opinion is important because it often influences the political process and affects the actions the government takes.

# Key Terms

**public opinion**  the aggregation of views shared by a segment of society on issues of interest or concern to people

**public policy**  the choices the government makes and the actions it takes in response to a particular issue or problem

**political socialization**  the process by which people acquire political beliefs

**mass media**  any means of communication that provides information to a large audience

**propaganda**  information designed to influence public opinion

**poll**  a survey of people scientifically selected to provide opinions about something

**sample**  the group of people who take part in a poll

**sampling error**  the margin of error that indicates a poll's accuracy

**bias**  errors introduced by polling methods that lead to one outcome over others

**objectivity**  freedom from bias and outside factors that may influence the results of a poll

**exit poll**  a poll that surveys a randomly selected fraction of voters after they have voted

# Taking Notes

As you read, take notes on factors that shape public opinion. Record your notes in the chart below.

| Factor | How it shapes public opinion |
|---|---|
|  |  |
|  |  |
|  |  |
|  |  |

# Section Summary

## WHAT IS PUBLIC OPINION?

**Public opinion** is the group of views shared by a segment of society on issues of interest to people. Public opinion is often divided and can focus on a variety of issues, ranging from the government's foreign policy to community problems.

**Public policy**, the choices the government makes and the actions it takes in response to an issue or problem, is related to public opinion. On the one hand, public policy can form public opinion, as Americans react to government actions. On the other hand, public opinion can form public policy. If enough Americans decide that a certain action needs to be taken, they can often convince government officials to make policy that addresses this need.

There are many ways Americans can express their individual and collective opinions. Voting is one example. People can also protest, write letters or blogs, or testify at public hearings. Additionally, people can join and support private organizations whose missions they respect and that work to influence policymakers.

> Imagine that you just voted in an election for governor. How did you share your beliefs by voting?
>
> _____
> _____
> _____
> _____

## FORMING PUBLIC OPINION

A number of factors can affect a person's **political socialization**, or the way a person acquires political beliefs. Family is an important factor, since children grow up listening to family members' beliefs on a range of political issues. School and work are two other factors that help shape the way a person feels about politics. Age, race, gender, and religion can further influence a person's opinions.

> Name three factors that shape a person's political beliefs.
>
> _____
> _____
> _____
> _____

## MEDIA AND PUBLIC OPINION

**Mass media**—any means of communication that provides information to a large audience—also influences public opinion. Newspapers, online news, and television news, all report on politics and issues that are important to both politicians and the public. Through coverage of an issue—or lack thereof—mass media can help shape the public agenda. However, as critics point out, mass media can sometimes be harmful, when there is bias in reporting or story selection, factual inaccuracy, or over consolidation of media outlets.

The earliest and longest-lasting form of mass media in the United States is print media, such as newspapers and magazines. Today, newspapers remain an important source of news and opinion, as do television, talk radio, and Internet news sites. It is now easier than ever to access news in very little time. Comparing information from multiple sources of news media helps people avoid **propaganda**, information purposely designed to shape public opinion.

> **Why is it important to receive news from more than one source?**
> _____
> _____
> _____
> _____

## MEASURING PUBLIC OPINION

A public opinion **poll** is a survey of people scientifically selected to provide opinions about something. When a poll is designed and conducted accurately, it can be an excellent gauge of public opinion.

The first step to ensuring accuracy in a poll is to pick an appropriate **sample**, or group of people who will take part in the poll. The size of the sample must be large enough to reflect the body of people the poll is supposed to represent, such as all registered voters. Additionally, the people who make up the sample must be chosen randomly. A well-designed scientific poll will also include questions that are worded in a way that does not unduly influence the respondent's answers. If a poll includes questions without **bias**, or polling method errors that lead to one outcome over others, it is more likely that the results of the poll will be **objective**—free from bias and other outside influences.

> **Explain the role of a sample in a poll.**
> _____
> _____
> _____
> _____

There is room for error in even the best designed poll. The **sampling error**, or margin of error in a poll, indicates a poll's accuracy and is given as a percent above and below the poll's results.

**Exit polls** are frequently used during elections. In these polls, voters are asked who they voted for, right after they vote. While these results can sometimes predict winners before elections are over, critics argue that they may discourage those who have not voted yet from voting and alter final results.

## The Political Process

**MAIN IDEA**
Interest groups are private organizations that try to influence public opinion and convince public officials to accept their goals and views. They give political power to segments of society that have similar views.

# Key Terms

**interest group** a collection of people who hold similar views and goals

**political action committee** an organization created to raise and contribute money legally to the campaigns of political candidates

**trade association** a type of business group that represents certain industries or parts of industries

**labor unions** organizations of workers who do the same job or work in related industries

**endorse** to publicly declare support for a candidate

**lobbying** contacting public officials to persuade them to support certain interests

**grass roots** the name given to the lowest level of an organization or society

# Taking Notes

As you read, take notes on the different types of interest groups. Record your notes in the graphic organizer below.

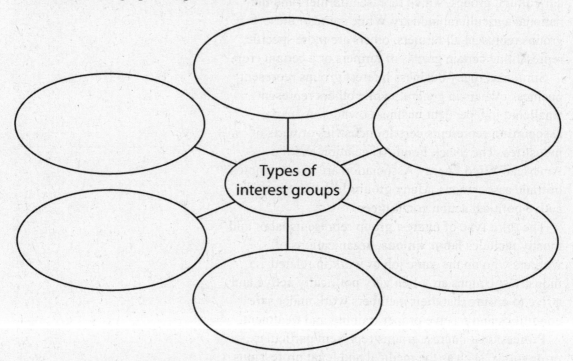

# Section Summary

## INTEREST GROUPS AND WHAT THEY DO

An **interest group** is a collection of people who hold similar views and goals. Interest groups have three main functions: organize people with common views, provide members with a way to participate in politics, and supply information about the group's views to policymakers and other members of the public. Interest groups often form **political action committees**, organizations whose purpose is to legally raise and contribute money to candidates whom members want to support.

For many Americans, interest groups provide a more powerful outlet for influencing public policy and the politicians behind it. While membership in interest groups has been lower in recent years, financial contributions to these groups have been higher. This monetary increase has helped interest groups extend their reach to a broad television and Internet audience.

> **How do interest groups give their members more of a political voice?**
>
> _____
>
> _____
>
> _____

## TYPES OF INTEREST GROUPS

There are six types of interest groups. The first type are agricultural groups, which represent farmers and the national agricultural industry While some of these groups represent all farmers, others are more specific, representing certain groups of farmers or a certain crop.

Similarly, many business interest groups represent business owners in general, while others represent small and independent business owners. A **trade association** represents certain industries or parts of industries. The Snack Food Association and the American Wind Energy Association are two examples of trade associations. Many groups like these include active political action committees.

The third type of interest group represents labor and mostly includes **labor unions**, organizations of workers who do the same job or work in related industries. Unions are often very politically active and strive to ensure that their members work under safe conditions and receive proper training and treatment.

Professional interest groups represent particular professions, such as the medical and legal professions. Professional groups typically educate the public about their specific profession, monitor training and licensing within the profession, and create a set of professional standards.

The fifth type of interest group is societal groups, organizations that represent certain religious, social, racial, and ethnic segments of the population. The National Organization of Women and the American Muslim Alliance are both examples of societal groups.

The last category of interest group is made up of cause-based groups, which focus on a particular cause rather than a segment of the U.S. population. Cause-based groups include Mothers Against Drunk Driving and the Center for Civic Education.

> **How are cause-based interest groups different from other interest groups?**
> _____
> _____
> _____

## HOW INTEREST GROUPS WORK

Interest groups work very hard to influence both public opinion and public policy. They **endorse**, or publicly declare support for, candidates who share their views and contribute to campaigns via political action committees. Interest groups also spend a great deal of time **lobbying**—contacting public officials to persuade them to support their members' interests. Providing people to testify at public hearings and summoning support at the **grass roots** level—the lowest level of an organization or society—are additional strategies. In the past, interest groups have also filed lawsuits on behalf of the population or cause they represent in order to influence public policy.

## INTEREST GROUPS AND THE PUBLIC GOOD

Interest groups affect the public good in different ways. For Americans not in the majority, be it due to their background, profession, or opinion, interest groups provide a way to be heard.

While interest groups can help protect minority interests, critics believe that they can have too much influence, especially when they are well funded. Critics further argue that the groups often focus too narrowly on an issue, rely too heavily on emotional appeals, and may prevent Congress from acting swiftly on issues. Congress has placed limits on interest groups and their relationship with legislators as recently as 2007, tightening ethics rules and lobbying opportunities.

> **What is one advantage of interest groups? What is one disadvantage?**
> _____
> _____
> _____
> _____

## The Political Process

**MAIN IDEA**
Political parties are formal organizations that work to elect candidates to public office. Our political system is dominated by two major parties, but other parties are actively involved in the system.

# Key Terms

**political party** an organization that tries to elect its members to public office so that its views can become public policy

**political spectrum** the continuum of general political beliefs

**nomination process** naming candidates for elective office

**electorate** the body of people entitled to vote

**one-party system** a party system in which a single political party controls government

**two-party system** a party system in which two major parties compete to control government

**multiparty system** a party system in which several parties compete for control

**third party** any political party in a two-party system besides the two major ones

**independent candidate** a candidate who is not associated with any party

**precinct** the smallest unit for administering elections and local voting

**ward** a voting district made up of several precincts

# Taking Notes

As you read, take notes on how political parties serve the public good. Record your notes in the graphic organizer below.

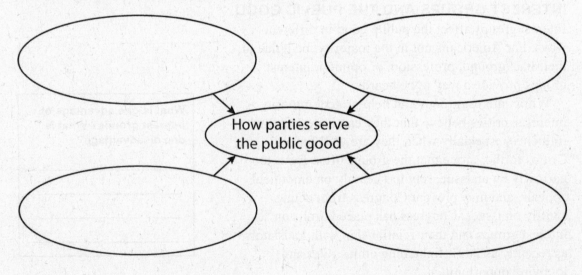

How parties serve the public good

# Section Summary

## THE ROLE OF POLITICAL PARTIES

A **political party** is an organization that tries to elect its members to public office in order to make its views public policy. Party members share similar ideas and views about society and government and unite these ideas in a political program called an ideology. What the ideology includes determines a party's place on the **political spectrum**, or the continuum of general political beliefs. For example, in the United States, the Democratic Party falls on the liberal end of the spectrum and the Republican Party on the conservative end.

Political parties have three roles within the political system. First, parties shape the **nomination process**, or the naming of candidates for public office, by identifying, and supporting candidates who share their views. Second, parties assist the electoral process by educating and motivating the **electorate**—the body of people entitled to vote—about issues and the voting process itself, making candidates more accessible by giving them a "brand name," and monitoring the actions of party and non-party policymakers. Finally, parties help determine the organization of government. The president typically nominates people who share his or her party's basic views, and Congress is controlled by the party that has the most members in each house.

> How are political parties involved in the political process after one of their candidates has been elected?
>
> _____
> _____
> _____
> _____

## THE AMERICAN TWO-PARTY SYSTEM

There are three types of party systems: one-party, two-party, and multiparty. In a **one-party system**, a single party controls government; if other parties are permitted to operate, they typically have little power. Likewise, in a **two-party system**, as in the United States, additional parties do exist but have limited influence on the electoral process. In a **multiparty system,** several parties compete for control, sometimes forming coalitions to create a majority.

The United States' two-party system dates back to the first American political parties, the Federalists and the Democratic-Republicans. While these parties ceased to exist during the early 1800s, the parties that formed from the remains of the Democratic-

> How is the competition within a multiparty system different than that in a two-party system?
>
> _____
> _____
> _____
> _____

Republican Party continue to be the most powerful in the country: the Democrats and Republicans. While **third parties**—any political party in a two-party system besides the two major ones—and **independent candidates**—those not affiliated with a party—can affect elections, the Democratic and Republican parties continue to wield the most influence within the electoral process.

## PARTY ORGANIZATION

Political parties are organized at the local, state, and national levels. At the local level, county parties identify and support local candidates, as well as organize support for candidates at higher levels. County parties are run by county committees, the members of which are elected by party members in county **precincts**—the smallest units for administering elections and local voting. Voting districts made up of several precincts are called **wards**.

At the state level, state committees composed of members of county committees work on supporting party candidates at the local, state, and national levels. A state chairperson leads these efforts.

At the national level, a committee made up of a national chairperson and members of state parties organizes major outreach and fundraising efforts for candidates at all levels. The national committee also creates and supports specific, affiliated organizations, such as the College Democrats of America or the National Teenage Republicans.

> **Does support for local candidates end at the county level? Explain.**
> _____
> _____
> _____

## POLITICAL PARTIES AND THE PUBLIC GOOD

Parties can benefit the political process by filtering out extreme ideas, building inclusive support for issues, providing political and social stability, discouraging short-term shifts in power, and giving voters a "brand-name" idea of who is running. However, by reaching out to so many segments of the population at once, parties can sometimes lack unity, discipline, and loyalty. Additionally, the monetary support that parties receive from interest groups often prompts critics to question whether elected officials are always acting in the public interest.

> **Explain three benefits of political parties.**
> _____
> _____
> _____

## The Political Process

**MAIN IDEA**
The Constitution creates a system in which citizens elect representatives to public office. Each citizen has the responsibility to help make this system work. Citizens can affect the electoral process in many ways, but the most powerful is by voting on election day.

# Key Terms

**hard money** money donated to an individual campaign

**soft money** money given to a party rather than to a specific candidate

**write-in candidates** candidates who ask voters to write in his or her name on a ballot

**caucus** a meeting of party members who select the candidates to run for election

**direct primary** election in which a party's candidates for office are chosen directly by voters

**closed primary** election in which only voters registered as party members may vote for that party's candidates

**open primary** election in which registered voters may vote for any party's candidates, as long as they only vote for one party

**plurality** when a candidate receives more votes than any other candidate in that election

**absentee ballot** a ballot submitted on or before election day by a voter who cannot be present on election day

# Taking Notes

As you read, take notes on some factors that may influence voter behavior. Record your notes in the graphic organizer below.

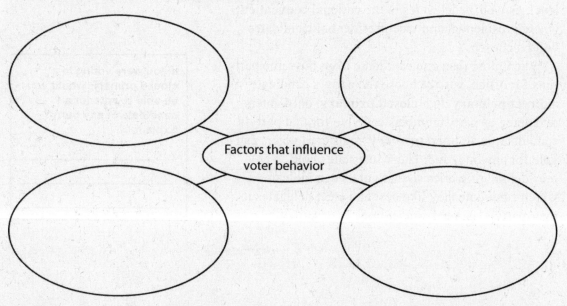

Factors that influence voter behavior

# Section Summary

## ORGANIZING AND FINANCING CAMPAIGNS

When running for office, candidates need to reach out to voters however possible, be it on television or by ringing doorbells. Doing all of this takes money. The candidate can raise money through his or her party, private individuals, personal or private funds, or political action committees. A **hard-money** contribution is money donated directly to a campaign. **Soft-money** contributions, created to get around the limits on hard money, are donations made to a candidate's party rather than directly to the candidate.

> **What is the difference between hard and soft money?**
> _____
> _____
> _____

## CHOOSING CANDIDATES

There are several ways that a candidate can get his or her name on the ballot. He or she can seek a party's nomination or run as an independent candidate, self-nominate by collecting signatures on a petition, or simply run as a **write-in candidate** by asking voters to write in his or her name on the ballot.

Candidates can also be chosen by a party caucus or convention. A **caucus** is a meeting of elected party delegates at which candidates are selected. Caucus members are elected during lower-level precinct caucuses, which are open to all party members. Conventions are completely open to the public, with delegates representing party members not present. Local and state conventions select candidates at their level, as well as delegates to the national convention, where presidential and vice-presidential candidates will be chosen.

When more than one candidate from the same party runs for office, voters choose the party's candidate in a **direct primary**. In a **closed primary**, only voters registered as party members can vote for that party's candidate; in an **open primary**, registered voters can vote for any one candidate. Most states hold presidential primaries so that voters can indicate which candidate they like best and elect delegates to their party's national convention.

> **If you were voting in a closed primary, would you be able to vote for a candidate of any party? Explain.**
> _____
> _____
> _____

## VOTING AND VOTING BEHAVIOR

Recently, voter turnout has ranged from less than two-thirds of voters in presidential elections to lower than 40 percent in state and local elections. One explanation for low turnout is that some people do not believe that their vote will make a difference. Another explanation may lie in the difficulty of registering to vote, the step one must take before actually voting.

When people do vote, there are four major factors that can influence the decisions they make: party identification, the voter's own views on issues, a candidate's personal and professional background, and the voter's background.

> **What two factors might be contributing to low voter turnout?**
>
> _____
>
> _____
>
> _____

## MORE ABOUT ELECTIONS

General elections take place at the end of campaigns. In most states, the candidate who receives a **plurality**, or more votes than any other candidates, wins the election. A few states hold runoff elections if no candidate receives a majority of the vote. Special elections are held when an officeholder has died or resigned.

Regardless of the type, most elections follow standard practices and all adhere to state and federal laws. Federal elections take place on the first Tuesday following the first Monday in November in even-numbered years. Most state and many local elections also take place on this day. On election day, voters go to their precinct polling place and cast a secret ballot, sometimes on paper and sometimes on machines.

If a voter knows he or she will be unable to vote on election day, whether due to illness, travel, or another reason, he or she can cast an **absentee ballot**, or in some states, vote earlier than election day.

> **Is a plurality of votes always the same as a majority of votes? Explain.**
>
> _____
>
> _____
>
> _____
>
> _____

## CAMPAIGNS AND THE PUBLIC GOOD

Political campaigns help voters become informed about both issues and candidates. However, some Americans feel that campaigns rely too heavily on short television ads, which can only share a very small amount of information and sometimes relay a distorted message to viewers. Negative ads also bother some people, who prefer candidates to explain their own views instead of attacking those of others.

**Civil Liberties**

# Chapter Summary

## COMPREHENSION AND CRITICAL THINKING

Use information from the graphic organizer to answer the following questions.

1. **Describe** What does the Bill of Rights protect?

_____

_____

2. **Identify Cause and Effect** Due process of law ensures that the laws and procedures the government uses when prosecuting a person are fair. How do you think due process helps both accused persons and victims?

_____

_____

_____

3. **Evaluate** The Bill of Rights protects the fundamental freedoms of religion, speech, the press, assembly, and petition. Choose one of these freedoms and explain in your own words why the adjective *fundamental* applies to it.

_____

_____

_____

## Civil Liberties

**MAIN IDEA**
The United States was formed out of a belief that individuals had certain important liberties and rights. The Constitution's Bill of Rights protects these liberties and rights.

# Key Terms

**civil liberties** basic freedoms to think and act that all people have and that are protected against government abuse

**civil rights** rights of fair and equal status and treatment and the right to participate in government

**due process** following established and complete legal procedures

**incorporation doctrine** the Supreme Court's reasoning for incorporating much of the Bill of Rights into the Fourteenth Amendment; holds that certain protections are essential to due process of the law

# Taking Notes

As you read, take notes on how the Bill of Rights protects Americans' civil liberties and rights. Record your notes in the graphic organizer below.

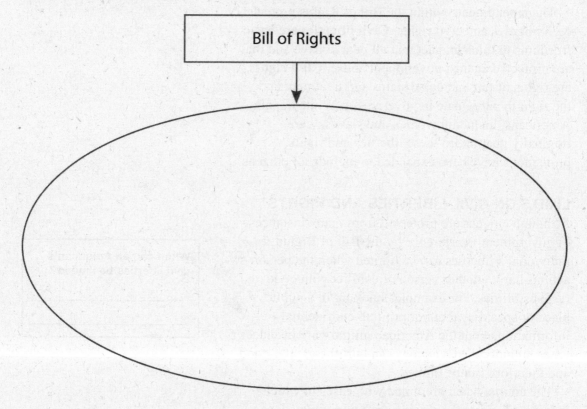

Bill of Rights

# Section Summary

## THE BILL OF RIGHTS

The Constitution did not originally include the Bill of Rights. After gaining independence from Great Britain, the states adopted their own individual constitutions, the majority of which protected individual freedoms and rights. Although Virginian delegate George Mason proposed a bill of rights at the Constitutional Convention, his idea was defeated by others' arguments that the state constitutions and a separation of powers were sufficient.

Yet it soon became clear that not all of the states would ratify the Constitution without at least the prospect of a bill of rights. Supporters of the Constitution finally agreed to add one as soon as the new government met, and in 1789, James Madison drafted a number of amendments. After much debate, Congress settled on 10 amendments—which listed specific rights yet did not deny any other rights—that were ratified and formally made part of the Constitution in 1791.

The amendments within the Bill of Rights protect civil liberties and civil rights. **Civil liberties** are basic freedoms to think and act that all people have and that are protected against government abuse. **Civil rights** are rights of fair and equal status and treatment and the right to participate in government. While not all Americans, including women and slaves, were originally guaranteed these liberties and rights, protections have been expanded to include all citizens.

> Does the Bill of Rights limit Americans' rights to only those listed within it? Explain.
>
> _____
>
> _____

## LIMITS ON CIVIL LIBERTIES AND RIGHTS

Although citizens are protected from many instances of government interference by the Bill of Rights, an individual's liberties can be limited when the person's actions harm another person or conflict with civic responsibilities. For example, smoking in a public place or speaking about or printing confidential information about the American military are instances when an individual's actions can hurt the greater good and therefore can be limited.

The courts, when presented with cases in which individuals claim their rights are being violated, can issue rulings that set a standard for how to balance

> When can an American's civil liberties be limited?
>
> _____
>
> _____

personal freedoms with the protection of all
Americans. Most of these rulings have occurred since
the early 1900s, and many are the result of cases
brought to the courts' attention by interest groups,
such as the National Association for the Advancement
of Colored People (NAACP) and the American Civil
Liberties Union (ACLU).

## CIVIL LIBERTIES AND THE FOURTEENTH AMENDMENT

The Bill of Rights protects individuals from some
actions by the federal government, not state and local
governments. However, over the years, the Supreme
Court has applied many of the protections within the
Bill of Rights to state and local governments, based on
the Fourteenth Amendment. This amendment, passed
after the Civil War to protect the rights of formerly
enslaved African Americans, forbids the states to
deprive anyone of life, liberty, or property without
**due process**—following established and complete
legal procedures. The Court established the
**incorporation doctrine** to justify merging much of
the Bill of Rights with the Fourteenth Amendment,
claiming that certain protections are essential to due
process of the law.

> **Why was the incorporation doctrine established?**
> _____
> _____

This incorporation has taken place little by little.
The first case to merge the Bill of Rights was
*Chicago, Burlington & Quincy Railroad* v. *Chicago*.
In this 1897 case, the Court ruled that the Fifth
Amendment's "just compensation" clause also applied
to the states. Later cases incorporated First
Amendment freedoms, the Sixth Amendment, and
parts of the Fourth, Fifth, and Eighth Amendments.

## Civil Liberties

**MAIN IDEA**
The First Amendment protects five fundamental freedoms that are central to the American notion of liberty: the freedoms of religion, speech, the press, assembly, and petition.

# Key Terms

**establishment clause** the part of the First Amendment that declares that government cannot take actions that create an official religion or support one religion over another

**free exercise clause** the part of the First Amendment that guarantees each person the right to hold any religious beliefs he or she chooses

**slander** a spoken defamatory statement

**libel** a printed defamatory statement

**treason** the crime of making war against the United States or giving "aid and comfort" to its enemies

**sedition** a legal term for speech or actions that inspire revolt against the government

**prior restraint** government action that seeks to prevent materials from being published

**symbolic speech** the communication of actions through symbols and actions

**freedom of association** the right to join with others, share ideas, and work toward a common purpose

# Taking Notes

As you read, take notes on the five freedoms protected by the First Amendment. Record your notes in the graphic organizer below.

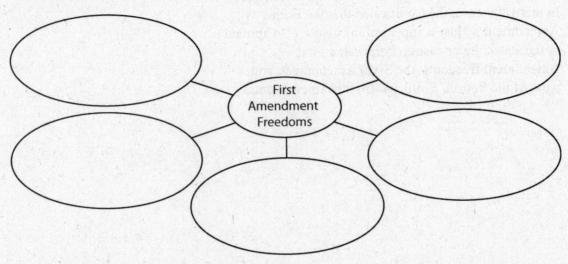

First Amendment Freedoms

# Section Summary

## RELIGIOUS FREEDOM

The First Amendment freedom of religion guarantees two things. First, the government cannot establish an official religion or support one religion over another—this is the part of the First Amendment called the **establishment clause**. This clause created the separation of church and state, a thorny issue that the federal courts have dealt with a on a case-by-case basis. Many past cases have deal with government-sponsored religious displays. Several other important cases have involved how the establishment clause relates to education. For example, the Court has carefully examined how public funds should be used in relation to private schools, which can include religious schools. Justices have also struck down mandatory morning prayer and silent meditation in public schools, eventually developing the Lemon Test in 1971. Since then, the Court considers a law constitutional if it has a secular purpose, if its major effects neither advance nor inhibit religion, and if it does not encourage "excessive government entanglement with religion."

The second part of the First Amendment related to freedom of religion is the **free exercise clause**, which guarantees each person the right to hold any religious beliefs they choose—but does not allow them to practice these beliefs however that way. In recent decades, the Court has mainly ruled religious practices illegal only when the interest of enforcing a law is very strongly justified by the needs of society.

> **What does the establishment clause prevent?**
> _____
> _____

## FREEDOM OF SPEECH AND OF THE PRESS

The First Amendment freedoms of speech and of the press allow Americans to participate in the democratic process with little fear of punishment by the government. These freedoms also make it possible for Americans to watch their government debate and act, as well as access most government documents.

While the freedom of speech protects most speech, including that which is racist or offensive, the government can limit obscene speech or printed materials, in addition to speech and printed materials that knowingly harm another person. These types of

> **How does freedom of speech give Americans access to politicians?**
> _____
> _____

speech and printed materials include instances of
**slander**—a spoken defamatory statement—and
**libel**—a printed defamatory statement. Also,
**sedition**—a legal term for speech or actions that
inspire revolt against the government—or speech or
writings that are considered examples of **treason**—the
crime of making war against the United States or
giving "aid and comfort" to its enemies—can be
prohibited. The Supreme Court and the country as a
whole have struggled with what constitutes seditious
speech and how to define "clear and present danger"
when evaluating the consequences of such speech

Freedom of the press helps the spread of
information in a democratic society. The government
regulates television and radio more closely than other
media forms. Historically, print media has mostly
been protected from **prior restraint**, or government
action that seeks to prevent materials from being
published. The Supreme Court has repeatedly ruled
that prior restraint can only be used when the
government can prove how the potentially printed
materials can cause immediate harm. Likewise, the
Court has ruled that **symbolic speech**, or the
communication of ideas through symbols and actions,
falls under the protection of the First Amendment
unless it threatens property or public order.

> **Explain prior restraint in your own words.**
> _____
> _____

## FREEDOMS OF ASSEMBLY AND PETITION

The First Amendment freedoms of assembly and
petition allow Americans to meet and share ideas, as
well as create initiatives, or petitions designed to force
the government to consider an issue or allow a vote.
Various Supreme Court cases have confirmed these
two freedoms, even incorporating the right to
assembly into the Fourteenth Amendment. While the
government can almost never limit the content of an
assembly, it can restrict when, where, and how some
assemblies are held. The Supreme Court has also ruled
that while the **freedom of association**, or the right to
join with others, share ideas, and work toward a
common purpose, is not explicitly stated in the
Constitution, it is established simply by the presence
of the other First Amendment freedoms and the due
process clause.

> **What power does the government have over assemblies?**
> _____
> _____

Name _____ Class _____ Date _____

# Civil Liberties

**MAIN IDEA**
A key purpose of the Bill of Rights is to protect individuals from government abuses. Several amendments limit the government's power and protect individual rights against government actions.

## Key Terms

**probable cause** the strong likelihood that a search would find evidence of a crime

**search warrant** a document that gives police legal authority to search private property

**exclusionary rule** the rule that evidence obtained illegally may not be used against a person in court

**police power** the government's ability to regulate behavior for the common good

**procedural due process** legal expectation that government follow certain procedures before punishing a person

**substantive due process** legal expectation that laws are fair and just

## Taking Notes

As you read, take notes on the different amendments discussed in this section. Record your notes in the graphic organizer below.

| Amendment | Protections |
|-----------|-------------|
| Second | |
| Third | |
| Fourth | |
| Fifth | |

# Section Summary

## THE RIGHT TO KEEP AND BEAR ARMS

The Second Amendment was included in the Bill of Rights to allow states to form their own militias and to relieve Americans' fears of an overly powerful, federally-controlled standing army. Today, Americans continue to debate the true meaning of the amendment. Gun-rights advocates claim that it gives individuals the right to own whatever guns they choose. Gun-control advocates claim that nothing in the amendment prevents the government from limiting gun ownership. With the exception of one case in which it upheld a law restricting the possession of certain guns, the Supreme Court has left decisions about gun laws to the lower courts.

> **What was the original purpose of the Second Amendment?**
>
> _____
>
> _____

## SECURITY OF HOME AND PERSON

The Third Amendment forbids the government from housing troops in private homes during peacetime without the owner's consent—the Constitution's response to earlier practices by the British army.

As with the Third Amendment, the Fourth Amendment, which forbids "unreasonable searches and seizures," was inspired by colonial British practices, such as conducting searches without **probable cause**, or reasonable grounds. The Fourth Amendment requires probable cause for **search warrants**, documents that give police legal authority to search public property. Fourth Amendment protections also limit police to searching only for evidence related to a crime they are investigating, allowing them to take other evidence only when it is in "plain view." In response to searches conducted illegally, the Supreme Court has established the **exclusionary rule**, which states that evidence obtained illegally may not be used against a person in court. However, this rule does not apply to police searches conducted outside or in a person's trash.

> **What does the exclusionary rule prevent?**
>
> _____
>
> _____

Stopping a person who is walking down the street or in a car in order to search them is legally considered a seizure, and is justifiable if police believe there is reasonable suspicion that the person may harm others. But under the protections of the Fourth Amendment, there must be probable cause to arrest

the person. Also, in order to search a car, police need
to first stop the driver based on probable cause, such
as a traffic violation. Any evidence then found during
the search is allowable.

Other modern-day Fourth Amendment issues
include how much freedom government agencies have
to monitor electronic communications without
warrants—especially since the passage of the USA
PATRIOT Act—and which public and private
employers can drug test their employees and when.
The Supreme Court has ruled that schools may
randomly drug test students, a segment of the
American population that has fewer Fourth
Amendment rights. For example, students and their
belongings can be searched without probable cause.

## THE RIGHT TO PRIVACY

While the right to privacy is not explicitly stated in the
Constitution, many Americans and, at times, the
Supreme Court feel that citizens are entitled to the
right in certain situations. Some arguments point to
the expectation of privacy built into the Fourth
Amendment, as well as the guarantee of liberty in the
due process clauses of the Fifth and Fourteenth
Amendments. In the landmark cases *Griswold* v.
*Connecticut* (1965) and *Roe* v. *Wade* (1973), the
Supreme Court ruled that certain amendments indicate
a "zone of privacy" and a right to privacy that can
protect some decisions and behaviors.

> What is one way the right to privacy has been established, even though it is not mentioned in the Constitution?
>
> _____
>
> _____

## DUE PROCESS OF LAW

The concept of due process is inherent in both the
Fifth Amendment, which applies due process to the
federal government, and the Fourteenth Amendment,
which applies it to state governments. Due process
limits the government's **police power**, or ability to
regulate behavior for the common good. **Procedural
due process** requires that government follow certain
procedures before punishing a person. **Substantive
due process** requires that the laws potentially used to
punish a person are fair and just. Either right can be
limited in cases where the government's need to do
something is strongly justified and is in the interest of
the greater good.

> What is the difference between procedural and substantive due process?
>
> _____
>
> _____

## Civil Liberties

**MAIN IDEA**
The Constitution contains many features that help ensure that people accused of a crime receive fair and reasonable treatment—from arrest to trial to punishment.

# Key Terms

**civil law** category of law that covers private disputes between people over property and relationships

**criminal law** category of law that deals with crimes and their punishments

**indictment** a formal complaint of criminal wrongdoing issued by a grand jury

**bail** money pledged by the accused as a guarantee that he or she will return to court for trial

**capital punishment** punishment by death

**Miranda warnings** a list of certain constitutional rights possessed by those accused of crimes

**bench trial** a trial in which the judge alone hears and decides a case

**double jeopardy** restriction on trying a person twice for the same offense

# Taking Notes

As you read, take notes on the protected rights of people accused of crimes. Record your notes in the graphic organizer below.

```
┌─────────────────────────────┐        ┌─────────────────────────────┐
│                             │        │                             │
│   Rights of the Accused     │ ─────▶ │                             │
│                             │        │                             │
└─────────────────────────────┘        └─────────────────────────────┘

┌─────────────────────────────┐        ┌─────────────────────────────┐
│                             │        │                             │
│                             │ ─────▶ │                             │
│                             │        │                             │
└─────────────────────────────┘        └─────────────────────────────┘

┌─────────────────────────────┐        ┌─────────────────────────────┐
│                             │        │                             │
│                             │ ─────▶ │                             │
│                             │        │                             │
└─────────────────────────────┘        └─────────────────────────────┘
```

# Section Summary

## THE U.S. JUSTICE SYSTEM

There are two categories of law: civil and criminal. **Civil law** involves private disputes between people over property or relationships. Subcategories of civil law include contract law, tort law, property law, and family law. Civil lawsuits can be settled by trial, mediation, arbitration, or negotiation. When civil lawsuits do go to trial, they typically follow five basic steps: the plaintiff hires a lawyer and files a complaint, the two sides try to settle the dispute before the trial begins, the two sides exchange information in discovery, a judge or jury hears the trial, and the judge or jury issues a ruling, which may be appealed later.

    **Criminal law** is the system for dealing with crimes—both misdemeanors and felonies—and their punishments. In most federal criminal cases, per the Fifth Amendment, an accused person faces a grand jury. If it believes there is enough evidence of a crime, the grand jury issues an **indictment**, or formal complaint of criminal wrongdoing. Once an indictment is issued, the accused is arrested, goes through hearings, and may be allowed to temporarily go free by posting **bail**, or money pledged by the accused as a guarantee that he or she will return to court for trial. If the accused pleads guilty or accepts a plea bargain, he or she will be sentenced without a trial. If the accused pleads not guilty, a trial takes places, after which sentencing occurs if the person is found guilty. The harshest sentence is **capital punishment**, or punishment by death.

| What are two different ways plaintiffs and defendants can settle civil lawsuits? |
| --- |
| _____ |
| _____ |

| What takes place first: sentencing or trial? |
| --- |
| _____ |

## RIGHTS OF THE ACCUSED

In the American justice system, a person accused of a crime is presumed innocent until proven guilty and afforded several protections under the Constitution. First, by almost never allowing the government to suspend the writ of habeas corpus, the Constitution ensures that the accused will have a chance to defend his or her actions in court. Second, under the Fifth Amendment, the accused needs to first be indicted by a grand jury before standing trial for most federal crimes. Third, the Fifth Amendment also prevents the accused from being forced to give spoken evidence of or testify about anything that suggests his or her own guilt. In response to violations of this third protection, police must now read the **Miranda warnings**, or list of constitutional rights possessed by the accused, to suspects before they are arrested.

The Constitution does not provide any protections for victims of crime. In recent years, several states have passed such laws, including some that give victims the right to be informed of related offenders' convictions, sentences, imprisonment, and release.

> **What do the Miranda warnings tell accused persons?**
>
> _____
> _____
> _____

## GUARANTEES OF A FAIR TRIAL

The Sixth Amendment guarantees the right of Americans accused of a crime to a "speedy and public trial" and applies to both the federal government and the states. Delays that harm a defendant or give a prosecutor undue advantage can violate the Sixth Amendment. A "public" trial is considered one that is open to the public, although the court may limit press and public access in certain circumstances.

The Sixth Amendment also guarantees those accused of criminal charges the right to a trial by an impartial and local jury; a **bench trial**—one in which a judge alone hears and decides a case—may take place in specific situations. Additional Sixth Amendment—and Fourteenth Amendment— protections include the right to be informed of charges, the right to confront witnesses, and the right to an adequate, professional defense. Furthermore, the Fifth Amendment prohibits **double jeopardy**, or trying a person twice for the same offense.

> **Is a jury involved in a bench trial? Explain.**
>
> _____
> _____
> _____

## PUNISHMENT

Americans convicted of crimes are also protected. The Eighth Amendment prohibits the government from imposing excessive fines; this protection does not apply to civil cases between private parties. The Eighth Amendment also bans "cruel and unusual punishment," the definition of which has mainly been left to the lower courts, particularly in cases involving capital punishment. Most states allow the death penalty, which the Supreme Court has declared constitutional, but only when applied to criminals fairly.

## Civil Rights

# Chapter Summary

## COMPREHENSION AND CRITICAL THINKING

Use information from the graphic organizer to answer the following questions.

1. **Describe** What was the result of the U.S. civil rights movement?

   _____

   _____

2. **Explain** Why is the idea behind the equal protection clause so important?

   _____

   _____

3. **Elaborate** American culture needed to change before all Americans were guaranteed the same civil rights. How do you think the civil rights movement helped these changes come about?

   _____

   _____

## Civil Rights

**MAIN IDEA**
The Constitution is designed to guarantee basic civil rights to everyone. The meaning of civil rights has changed over time, and many groups have been denied their civil rights at different times in U.S. history.

## Key Terms

**prejudice** a negative opinion formed without just grounds

**racism** discrimination and unfair treatment based on race

**reservation** an area of public land set aside by the government for Native Americans

**Japanese American internment** the mandatory relocation of all people of Japanese descent on the West Coast to War Relocation Centers in 1942

## Taking Notes

As you read, take notes on the meaning and importance of civil rights and on how discrimination has affected different groups. Record your notes in the graphic organizer below.

| Civil Rights | Discrimination |
|---|---|
| | |

# Section Summary

## CIVIL RIGHTS IN THE UNITED STATES

Civil rights are rights that involve equal status and treatment. They protect people from discrimination, the act or practice of treating people unfairly based on their race, national origin, sex, religion, age, or other factors. Civil rights also give people the right to participate in government, such as voting and running for office.

In the United States, civil rights are protected by the law. Such laws are found in the Constitution and its amendments, federal and state laws, and Supreme Court decisions. However, for long periods of U.S. history, the government and much of American society did not consider certain groups entitled to guaranteed civil rights. Society's idea of fair and equal treatment has changed over the years, and women and ethnic and racial minorities have successfully fought for the rights to vote, participate in government, and be free from discrimination.

> **What American laws protect civil rights?**
> _____
> _____

## A PATTERN OF DISCRIMINATION

In past centuries, the U.S. government operated with **prejudice**—a negative opinion formed without just grounds—toward certain groups. Such prejudice is primarily based on feelings of **racism**, or discrimination and unfair treatment based on race.

Enslaved for over 250 years, African Americans received horrible treatment for a good part of U.S. history. Until the 1860s, government and society considered them property and therefore unequal to white Americans. After the Civil War, the Thirteenth Amendment abolished slavery. This action was quickly followed by the passage of the Fourteenth and Fifteenth Amendments, which granted former slaves citizenship and the right to vote. Yet African Americans continued to suffer unfair treatment for decades, as attacks, new state laws, and court rulings produced new forms of discrimination.

Native Americans were long considered a group outside of American society and the protections of civil rights. Throughout the 1800s, the U.S. government consistently violated land treaties it made with Native Americans, eventually forcing them from

> **Why did the Thirteenth, Fourteenth, and Fifteenth Amendments fail to give adequate protection to African Americans?**
> _____
> _____
> _____

their traditional lands onto **reservations**, areas of public lands set aside by the government for Native Americans. Furthermore, Native Americans were often prevented from speaking their native languages, raising their own children, or following their traditional ways of life.

Asian Americans have also had to deal with discrimination, starting with the arrival of Chinese immigrants in the mid-1800s. As these immigrants took jobs in the mining and railroad industries, many Americans became angry about increased competition for jobs and discriminated against the Chinese in employment, housing, and access to public services. Chinese immigration was even temporarily banned in 1882. Similarly, Japanese immigration was halted in the early 1900s. Japanese Americans also experienced one of the worst violations of civil rights in U.S. history during an event known as **Japanese American internment**, when all people of Japanese descent on the West Coast were forced into War Relocation Centers from 1942 until the end of World War II.

> **Explain how Japanese American internment violated people's civil rights.**
>
> _____
>
> _____
>
> _____

Hispanics or Latinos—people with a Spanish-speaking background—are yet another group that has faced discrimination. As the United States took control of various lands where Hispanics lived, such as Texas and California, it treated the native people—now known as Mexican Americans—with disrespect, sometimes taking their land or segregating them. From the mid-1800s until modern times, several waves of Hispanic immigration have taken place, each of which has had to deal with the problem of discrimination.

Finally, women were denied equal treatment for years, as much of society—and the Supreme Court—considered them members of the "domestic sphere" only. Until 1920, when they won the right to vote, women could not actively participate in government, serve on juries, hold property or custody rights equal to men's, or pursue most educational and career opportunities.

## Civil Rights

**MAIN IDEA**
The Fourteenth Amendment was designed to bolster civil rights by requiring states to guarantee freed slaves "the equal protection of the laws." However, African Americans and women still struggled to win equal treatment in American society.

# Key Terms

**equal protection clause** clause within the Fourteenth Amendment that requires states to apply the law the same way for one person that they would for another person in the same circumstances

**suspect classification** a classification based on race or national origin

**segregation** the separation of racial groups

**Jim Crow laws** segregation laws that reduced participation in government by African Americans

**separate-but-equal doctrine** the policy that laws requiring separate facilities for racial groups were legal so long as the facilities were "equal"

**suffrage** the right to vote

**Seneca Falls Convention** the first women's rights convention in the United States

**de jure segregation** segregation by law

**desegregation** ending the formal separation of groups based on race

**de facto segregation** segregation in fact, even without laws that require segregation

# Taking Notes

As you read, take notes on the meaning of equal protection and its effects on the struggles of African Americans and women for equal rights. Record your notes in the graphic organizer below.

# Section Summary

## EQUAL PROTECTION OF THE LAW

The **equal protection clause** in the Fourteenth Amendment requires states to apply the law the same way for one person that they would for another person in the same circumstances. Passed after the Civil War to protect the rights of former slaves, the Fourteenth Amendment was the first addition to the Constitution specifically designed to protect people from abuses by state governments.

Yet the equal protection clause does not always require people to be considered equal. The government can sometimes make a reasonable distinction between groups. The courts consider three guidelines when evaluating reasonable distinction. First, they may use the rational basis test, which allows the government to treat groups differently if the law in question is proven to accomplish a legitimate goal, such as public safety. A higher standard to determine reasonable distinction—especially in cases involving gender—is the intermediate scrutiny test, which requires a compelling reason and "exceedingly persuasive justification." Finally, the strict scrutiny test is used when a fundamental right is restricted or when a classification is made based on race or national origin, known as a **suspect classification**. It is very difficult for a distinction to pass this test, which has been used in cases involving interracial marriages and Japanese American internment.

> **What does the equal protection clause prevent from happening?**
>
> _____
>
> _____

## LAWS AND SEGREGATION AFTER THE CIVIL WAR

After the Civil War, the states ratified the Thirteenth Amendment, which banned slavery, the Fourteenth Amendment, which gave former slaves citizenship and required states to guarantee due process and equal protection, and the Fifteenth Amendment, which gave the right to vote to African American men. Congress also passed a series of civil rights laws that were supposed to protect other basic rights.

However, once military occupation of the South ended, so did much of the progress made by African Americans. Many states passed laws instituting

> **Did the Fifteenth Amendment give all African Americans the right to vote? Explain.**
>
> _____
>
> _____

segregation—the separation of racial groups—known as **Jim Crow laws** after a popular racist song. These laws targeted almost all areas of life, from participating in government to eating in restaurants. The Supreme Court upheld many Jim Crow laws, first ruling the Civil Rights Act of 1875 unconstitutional and then establishing—in *Plessy* v. *Ferguson* (1896)—the **separate-but-equal doctrine**, the policy that laws requiring separate facilities for racial groups were legal so long as the facilities were "equal."

## VOTING RIGHTS FOR WOMEN

While fighting for equal rights for African Americans, many women in the North began to demand equal rights for themselves, especially **suffrage**, or the right to vote. The first U.S. women's rights convention was the **Seneca Falls Convention**, where delegates called for a number of rights and adopted the Declaration of Sentiments. Upset that the Fifteenth Amendment did not also give women the right to vote, women continued to fight for suffrage throughout the 1800s. Although many western states and territories gave women suffrage by the late 1800s, the women's rights movement experienced little progress at the federal level. Finally, in 1920, the Nineteenth Amendment was ratified, which granted women the right to vote.

> Was the fight for women's suffrage more successful at the state or federal level in the 1800s?
>
> _____
>
> _____

## ROLLING BACK SEGREGATION

**De jure segregation**, or segregation by law, continued well into the 1900s. African American activist groups began challenging segregation in court, first insisting that the "equal" in "separate but equal" be a reality. The courts soon found segregated facilities consistently unequal. In the 1954 landmark case *Brown* v. *Board of Education of Topeka, Kansas*, the Supreme Court overturned *Plessy* and declared segregation in public schools unconstitutional. Schools slowly began the process of **desegregation**, or ending the formal separation of groups based on race, although in many places whites resisted this change. Today, all segregation is illegal but **de facto segregation**, or segregation in fact if not law, still exists. Americans continue to work to overcome this challenge.

> What is the difference between de jure segregation and de facto segregation?
>
> _____
>
> _____
>
> _____

## Civil Rights

**MAIN IDEA**
In the 1950s and 1960s, an organized movement demanding civil rights changed American society and led to a series of new federal laws that protected the civil rights of African Americans and other groups.

## Key Terms

**civil rights movement** a mass movement in the 1950s and 1960s to guarantee the civil rights of African Americans

**civil disobedience** nonviolent refusals to obey the law as a way to advocate change

**poll tax** a tax levied on someone who wants to vote

**affirmative action** a policy that requires employers and institutions to provide opportunities for members of certain historically underrepresented groups

**reverse discrimination** discrimination against the majority group

**quota** a fixed number or percentage

## Taking Notes

As you read, take notes on the civil rights movement and how it led to new civil rights laws. Record your notes in the graphic organizer below.

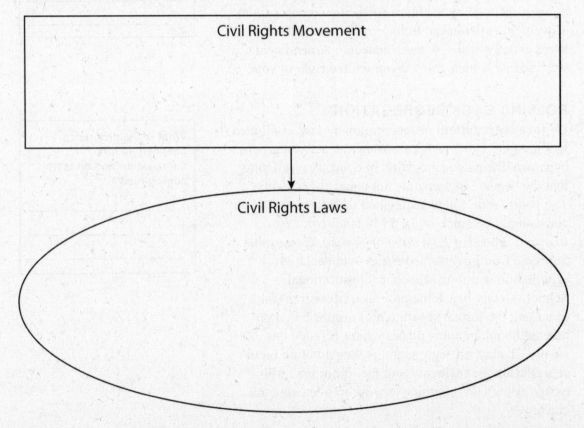

Civil Rights Movement

Civil Rights Laws

Name _____ Class _____ Date _____

Section 3 *continued*

# Section Summary

## THE CIVIL RIGHTS MOVEMENT

The **civil rights movement** was a mass movement in the 1950s and 1960s to guarantee the civil rights of African Americans. To communicate their message, members used acts of **civil disobedience**—nonviolent refusals to obey the law as a way to advocate change—such as sit-ins and boycotts. One of the most important boycotts of the movement involved civil rights leader Martin Luther King, Jr., and the Montgomery, Alabama, public buses, on one of which African American Rosa Parks refused to give up her seat to a white person. Parks' refusal and subsequent arrest led to the boycott and a Supreme Court ruling against the city that became the first major success of the civil rights movement. A 1963 March on Washington and the Selma to Montgomery marches also helped lead to the passage of laws that better protected the civil rights of minorities.

> **What is an example of an act of civil disobedience?**
> _____
> _____

## NEW FEDERAL LAWS

The strength of the civil rights movement inspired a series of new laws. The Civil Rights Act of 1957 included several federal anti-discrimination measures and created the Civil Rights Commission. The Civil Rights Act of 1960 let the federal government monitor places known for voter discrimination and made it illegal for anyone to restrict the right to vote. Both laws lacked enforcement strength, however, mainly due to the opposition of southerners in Congress.

The landmark Civil Rights Act of 1964 was much more powerful, passed under the authority of Congress's commerce clause. This legislation banned discrimination based on race, color, religion, sex, national origin—and, by 1967, age—in voting, employment, public accommodations, and government programs—and applied to individuals and businesses, not just actions by the states.

> **What kinds of discrimination did the Civil Rights Act of 1964 ban?**
> _____
> _____

Eventually the courts began to strike down unfair southern voting laws. Additionally, the Twenty-fourth Amendment banned **poll taxes**, taxes levied on someone who wants to vote. One year later, in 1965, the Voting Rights Act banned literacy tests and gave the federal government oversight power to change voting laws, voter registration, and elections anywhere Congress believed discrimination was widespread. However, in 2013, the Supreme Court ruled that it was unconstitutional to require federal approval for changes in voting laws.

## EXTENDING CIVIL RIGHTS

The civil rights era also resulted in extended civil rights for other minority groups. Various legislation and court rulings banned discrimination against women in many areas, including education and personal finance; required equal pay for men and women in the same jobs; and confirmed that women have a constitutional right to an abortion and that sexual harassment is illegal. Hispanics also saw improvements in treatment, especially in better application of the equal protection clause. The Voting Rights Act of 1975 made ballots available in Spanish, and migrant farm workers, many of whom were Hispanic, also gained new rights.

In the interest of Native Americans, Congress passed several laws, including some that allowed Native American groups more control over programs in their communities and confirmed their religious freedom. Finally, the Americans with Disabilities Act of 1990 required public buildings and transportation to be fully accessible and prohibited discrimination against people with disabilities.

> **What civil rights were extended to women as a result of the civil rights era?**
>
> _____
>
> _____

## AFFIRMATIVE ACTION

**Affirmative action** is a policy that requires employers and institutions to provide opportunities for members of certain historically underrepresented groups, first used in the 1960s to improve diversity in private and public workplaces. But by the late 1970s, some people claimed affirmative action policies were a form of **reverse discrimination**, or discrimination against the majority group. In 1978—in a case involving a **quota**, or fixed number or percentage, of minority students— and then again in 2003, the Supreme Court considered the role of affirmative action in higher education, ruling against the use of strict quota systems but declaring the use of race and diversity as factors in the admissions process constitutional. In some states, voters have passed ballot measures to restrict the use of affirmative action policies.

> **Explain in your own words why some people thought affirmative action was a form of reverse discrimination.**
>
> _____
>
> _____
>
> _____
>
> _____

**MAIN IDEA**
Being a U.S. citizen includes certain rights and responsibilities. The federal government regulates citizenship through its immigration and naturalization policies.

# Key Terms

**jus soli** a principle of citizenship by birthplace

**jus sanguinis** a principle of citizenship by parentage

**naturalization** the legal process by which an immigrant becomes a citizen

**denaturalization** the process through which a naturalized person loses citizenship

**expatriation** the legal process of giving up one's citizenship

**undocumented alien** someone living in a country without authorization from the government

**deportation** the legal process of forcing a noncitizen to leave a country

# Taking Notes

As you read, take notes on American citizenship and immigration issues.
Record your notes in the graphic organizer below.

| Citizenship | Immigration |
|---|---|
| | |

# Section Summary

## U.S. CITIZENSHIP

Both citizens and noncitizens—also known as aliens—are guaranteed civil rights in the United States, although aliens cannot vote. Most people become citizens by being born in the United States or a U.S. territory—a principle of citizenship by birth, called **jus soli**—or by being born on foreign soil to U.S. citizens—a principle of citizenship by parentage, called **jus sanguinis**.

**Naturalization** is the legal process by which an immigrant becomes a citizen. Naturalized citizens have all of the same rights as native-born citizens, although the Constitution does not allow them to become president or vice president. The naturalization process involves legal entry into the country; a period of residence in the country; the ability to read, write, and speak English; good moral character; belief in the Constitution; and positive feelings toward the country. Additionally, an exam and an oath are required. Also, there are some instances in which the government can grant collective naturalization to an entire group of people, such as when the United States gained new territories.

Although it is uncommon, a citizen can also lose his or her citizenship through a process called **denaturalization**. This is typically the result of becoming a citizen by fraud, by committing serious crimes against the U.S. government, or by working for or swearing allegiance to another country's government or military. In cases where a citizen willingly gives up citizenship, the legal process is called **expatriation**.

Americans share a civic identity in their devotion to American ideals, such as democracy, and to civic responsibilities, such as voting, respecting laws and others' rights, and paying taxes. Meeting civic responsibilities helps preserve and protect U.S. society.

> **What is the difference between a naturalized citizen and a person who received citizenship through jus soli?**
>
> _____
>
> _____
>
> _____

> **What are two examples of civic responsibilities?**
>
> _____
>
> _____

## IMMIGRATION POLICIES

Until the late 1800s, the U.S. government barely regulated immigration, often encouraging it instead. Once the U.S. population reached new heights and immigrants from outside of northern and western Europe began arriving in waves, American society and government became stricter about immigration. In 1875 Congress passed a law that barred entry to criminals, then a law that ended immigration from China—for 10 years—in 1882.

In the 1920s, new quota laws set the total number of legal immigrants at 165,000 a year, with quotas for specific European countries based on the national origin of the U.S. population in 1890. Immigration dropped as Asian, African, and Latin American immigrants were restricted. In 1965 the Immigration and Nationality Act Amendments—updated in 1990—abolished the quota system, set a new annual total, and gave preference to immigrants with certain skills or relatives in the United States. Today 675,000 immigrants are allowed per year, with many arriving from Asia and Latin America. Refugees and people seeking political asylum are subject to different immigration policies.

> **How did U.S. immigration policy change during the 1800s?**
>
> _____
>
> _____
>
> _____

## ILLEGAL IMMIGRATION

Illegal immigration is a major problem facing the United States. Most **undocumented aliens**, or unauthorized immigrants, have entered the country by crossing the U.S.-Mexico border or by overstaying legally issued visas. The government is unable to keep track of these approximately 11 million people, who are subject to **deportation**, or the legal process of forcing a noncitizen to leave the country, if caught. Some Americans feel that illegally entering the United States is wrong, and that illegal immigrants take away jobs from American citizens and strain government services. Others argue that illegal immigrants are just trying to build better lives for themselves and take otherwise undesirable jobs. The government has tried various tactics to stem illegal immigration, from creating and increasing the Border Patrol to granting one-time amnesty to undocumented aliens to making deportation easier. Yet officials still struggle over the problem and the best way to solve it.

> **What is one argument against illegal immigration? What is one argument in defense of illegal immigrants?**
>
> _____
>
> _____
>
> _____
>
> _____

## Understanding Elections

# Chapter Summary

| Candidates | Voters |
|---|---|
| • Work with staff to create message<br><br>• Deliver message via various media<br><br>• Raise funds from variety of sources<br><br>• Appeal to voters for support | • Educate selves about candidates and issues<br><br>• Register to vote and cast ballots<br><br>• Work on campaigns or at polls<br><br>• Run for office |

## COMPREHENSION AND CRITICAL THINKING

Use information from the graphic organizer to answer the following questions.

1. **Identify** Which duties do voters undertake in the election process?

_____

_____

2. **Draw Conclusions** How do you think different types of media outlets help candidates in different ways?

_____

_____

3. **Elaborate** Voting is considered the most basic form of political participation. Why do you think this is?

_____

_____

_____

## Understanding Elections

**READING FOCUS**
The purpose of election campaigns is to help the public learn about the candidates, so that voters can make an informed decision on election day. Candidates today take advantage of media exposure and polling in order to influence the voters and get elected to public office.

# Key Terms

**platform** a party's stand on important issues and the party's general principles

**focus group** a small gathering of people whose response to something is studied and used to predict the response of a larger population

**swing states** states where support for each candidate is about equal

**stump speech** a standard speech that candidates give during a campaign

**negative campaigning** attacking the opponent during a campaign

**sound bite** a very brief segment of a speech or statement

**demographic** a population group defined by a specific characteristic or set of characteristics

# Taking Notes

As you read the summaries, use your Student Casebook to take notes on the section.

# Case Study Summary

### TELEVISION AND THE 1960 ELECTION
The first televised presidential debates were held in 1960. Candidates Senator John F. Kennedy and Vice President Richard Nixon, whom voters already considered very different from one another, appeared in stark contrast during the debate. Kennedy looked tan and healthy, but Nixon looked tired and pale. While polls showed that people who had only listened to the debate on the radio thought had Nixon performed better, those who watched the debate claimed that Kennedy had won. The debate and its possible effect on the outcome of the election— Kennedy won by a slight margin—is still used today as an example of how powerful a role television plays in revealing a candidate's personality and overall public appeal.

# What You Need to Know Summary

## CAMPAIGN PLANNING

Candidates run campaigns to help the public get to know them and their **platform**, their party's stand on important issues and general principles. Running a campaign requires a dedicated, hard-working staff, the size of which can vary from campaign to campaign.

There are several key figures who work on campaigns. The campaign manager coordinates the entire campaign. He or she develops and executes the campaign plan and supervises other key staffers. The finance chair is charged with the responsibility of raising money to fund the campaign. The pollster creates scientific polls whose results then guide the direction of the campaign. The media coordinator arranges free and paid advertising to get the candidate's message to the public in as many ways possible. The scheduler manages the candidate's time to ensure that he or she attends the events necessary for a successful campaign. Issue advisers educate the candidate and write campaign position papers on major issues important to the voting public. The treasurer manages the money a campaign raises and spends. The volunteer coordinator recruits and manages volunteer staff. The press secretary creates press releases about the campaign and tracks media coverage. The speechwriter reviews and writes some of the candidate's speeches.

No matter what their role, staff members need to identify *how* and *where* they can make sure their candidate wins. Knowing this ahead of time helps a campaign develop and deliver their candidate's message. A large part of creating a winning message is knowing who will want to hear it, mainly by conducting polls and determining who is likely to vote for the candidate. Likewise, targeting the message to this select group of people is essential. Campaigns often use **focus groups**, small gatherings of people whose response to something is studied and used to predict the response of a larger population. Once a campaign staff knows how people feel about the candidate and the platform, they can "package" the candidate's image and create advertisements geared toward these feelings.

> **Why is it important that a candidate has a platform?**
>
> _____
> _____
> _____

> **What do focus groups tell campaign staff?**
>
> _____
> _____
> _____

## CONDUCTING A CAMPAIGN

Geography can help determine the direction a campaign takes. Presidential candidates will often spend more time in states with several electoral votes, in states where support for opponents is weak, or in **swing states**, those states where support for each candidate is about equal. Similarly, when visiting a state, a candidate is more likely to speak about those issues most important to the population. In addition to issue speeches, candidate regularly give **stump speeches**, or standard speeches delivered throughout the campaign.

Some of these speeches, as well as much of a candidate's advertising, may involve **negative campaigning**. When employing this strategy, a candidate attacks an opponent in hopes of decreasing his or her support and forcing the opponent to spend time and energy responding to the attack.

Whether negative or positive, advertising and other media coverage are among a campaign's key features. Television ads, interviews, and even simple photo opportunities are integral to a campaign's publicity. Radio spots and interviews can also be good publicity within a certain demographic. Campaign staff use newspapers to target older voters and the Internet to target younger voters, using both mediums to explain their candidate's message in greater depth.

One disadvantage of widespread media coverage, however, is the inability to control the **sound bites**, or brief segments of speeches or statements, that media might use. When used in a certain way, these sound bites can have a devastating or uplifting effect on a campaign.

Polls influence the direction of a campaign from start to finish. Early polls can identify **demographics**, or population groups defined by a specific characteristic or set of characteristics, that will or will not support a candidate. Polls also monitor public opinion and can potentially influence voter behavior.

> **What are two places candidates might speak in hopes of persuading voters?**
>
> _____
>
> _____

> **How can sound bites be dangerous to a campaign?**
>
> _____
>
> _____
>
> _____

# Simulation

Use your Student Casebook to help you complete the simulation.

**Undestanding Elections**

**READING FOCUS**
Money plays a major role in election campaigns. Candidates and their staff must carefully decide where the campaign will get money and how they will use this money.

# Key Terms

**Federal Election Commission** government agency created to enforce the Federal Election Campaign Act and administer the related public-funding program

**party-building activities** political party activities that do not support specific candidates

**issue ads** advertisements that support or oppose candidates' views without specifically calling for their election or defeat

**leadership PACs** groups formed by officeholders that are separate from the officeholders' campaign organizations

**527 group** a tax-exempt organization created to influence an election

# Taking Notes

As you read the summaries, use your Student Casebook to take notes on the section.

# Case Study Summary

## CONTROVERIES OVER CAMPAIGN FUNDING

In the early twenty-first century, two scandals involving members of Congress emphasized the need for campaign reform. In 2002 Ohio Representative James Traficant was found guilty of and convicted on 10 felony counts, some of which involved taking money donated to his campaign for personal use. Traficant was then expelled from the Senate by a vote of 420 to 1.

In 2005 Texas Representative Tom DeLay and one of his political action committees, TRMPAC, were indicted for making illegal campaign contributions. Delay had helped move corporate donations made to the National Republican Party to Republican candidates in Texas, where corporate contributions to state campaigns are illegal. After his indictment, Tom DeLay resigned from the House of Representatives.

> **How did Traficant and DeLay use campaign donations improperly?**
>
> _____
>
> _____
>
> _____

# What You Need to Know Summary

## FUNDING ELECTION CAMPAIGNS

Running an election campaign can be very expensive; currently, there is no limit in the United States on how much a candidate can spend. To raise money, candidates turn to four sources. First, candidates can accept individual donations. These donations are the largest funding source and only need to be reported if in excess of $200. Second, candidates can receive contributions from political action committees, or PACs. Third, the political party that a candidate represents can donate a limited amount of money. Finally, a presidential candidate can receive public funding, if he or she agrees to certain limits on any other money raised or spent.

In order to reduce the dependence of candidates on big donors, the government has initiated various campaign finance reforms. In the first half of the twentieth century, Congress banned corporations and labor unions from making campaign contributions. Then, in 1971, Congress passed the landmark Federal Election Campaign Act (FECA). This legislation established strict contribution limits and reporting responsibilities, created the current system of public funding for presidential campaigns, and instituted the **Federal Election Commission** (FEC) to enforce the FECA and administer the public funding program.

Congress amended the FECA multiple times during the 1970s, including a change in 1979 that allows parties to spend unlimited money on **party-building activities**—those that do not directly support candidates. This change in election law created a new kind of donation—soft money, or money not given directly to candidates. Unregulated by the FEC, soft-money donations are unlimited, can come from corporations, and often end up funding **issue ads**, which support or oppose candidates' views without specifically calling for their election or defeat.

Soft-money donations skyrocketed between 1996 and 2002, so much so that Congress passed legislation to curb it. The 2002 Bipartisan Campaign Reform Act (BCRA) banned soft-money contributions to political parties for advertising. However, in 2010, two Supreme Court decisions essentially allowed unlimited contributions and spending not made directly to candidates, parties, or other PACs.

> **What is a campaign's largest funding source?**
> _____
> _____

> **What is the difference between an individual donation to a campaign and soft money?**
> _____
> _____
> _____

## INTEREST GROUPS AND ELECTIONS

Since the role of interest groups in the campaign fundraising process is limited, it is up to the groups' PACs to collect money from members and donate it to specific campaigns. Donations to a national PAC are limited to $5,000 per year per donor, but many state PACs have no such limits. Similarly, **leadership PACs**, groups that officeholders can form to raise soft money, are also not subject to limits.

Critics of PACs question whether PAC donations give interest groups undue influence over candidates. But supporters point to the fact that interest-group members have more of a voice in the political process thanks to PACs.

**527 groups** are another source of campaign contributions. These groups are named for a section of the U.S. tax code that allows certain kinds of groups to pay no taxes. 527 groups, through a loophole in the 2002 BCRA, work to influence voters' opinions about candidates or issues. As long as a 527 is not directly connected to a candidate or party, it is allowed to raise and spend unlimited amounts of money without reporting its activities to the FEC. In the 2004 presidential campaigns, 527 groups mostly created ads that attacked a specific candidate, prompting a debate over the regulation of donations versus donors' freedom of speech.

Unlike 527s, campaign advertising is limited. The BCRA requires that all campaign media advertisements include a visual or oral message that identifies who is paying for the ad. If an ad comes directly from a campaign, the candidate must appear in the ad, along with audio of the candidate saying that he or she approves of the message.

> **What worries critics of PACs?**
> _____
> _____

> **How can you tell if a television advertisement comes directly from a campaign?**
> _____
> _____
> _____

# Simulation

Use your Student Casebook to help you complete the simulation.

## Understanding Elections

### READING FOCUS
Voting is one of the main responsibilities of U.S. citizenship. Being a part of the voting process and taking an active role in electing public officials helps give all Americans a voice in their government.

## Key Terms

**poll workers** people hired by local election officials to manage voting on election day

**poll watchers** volunteers whom a party or candidate sends to polling places to ensure that elections are being run fairly

**redistricting** the process of drawing new boundaries for legislative districts

## Taking Notes

As you read the summaries, use your Student Casebook to take notes on the section.

## Case Study Summary

### ELECTION 2000

In the 2000 presidential election, the race between Republican George W. Bush and Democrat Al Gore was so close that the result would depend upon who won Florida's 25 electoral votes. Yet the Florida race itself was so close that a recount was called in order to count every ballot once again.

When the recount was complete, results showed that Bush had won by about 1,500 votes. Democrats objected, claiming that the recount machines could not always accurately read the ballots, which Florida voters cast by punching a hole in them. Democrats then demanded a recount by hand, which Republicans opposed.

Both sides took their case to the Florida Supreme Court, which ordered the hand recount on December 8. The Bush campaign appealed the ruling to the U.S. Supreme Court, which ruled 5—4 on December 12 that the Florida court's ruling was unconstitutional. In the majority opinion, justices explained that the Florida court did not include standards for how votes should be recounted. The Court also declared that there was not enough time to resolve the controversy according to a deadline set by Florida law. Al Gore publicly accepted defeat on December 9.

> **Why did Democrats demand a hand recount in Florida during the 2000 presidential election?**
>
> _____
> _____
> _____

# What You Need to Know Summary

## POLITICAL PARTICIPATION

In a democratic republic, where political power belongs to the people, citizen participation is essential. Voting is a basic, extremely important form of participation. However, millions of eligible Americans choose not to vote, despite the fact that segments of the U.S. population struggled for years to win the right to vote.

Several factors might explain low voter turnout. First, the type of election affects voting. Presidential elections traditionally attract more voters than state elections and local elections. Age is another factor—older Americans are much more likely to go to the polls than those under the age of 25. Third, not all voters are aware of the impact of their individual vote. As the 2000 presidential election proved, there are times when every vote does count, particularly in local elections, where the outcome of often very close races has an impact on everyday life.

Besides voting, citizens can participate in the political process by volunteering to support campaigns, or to support or oppose specific issues. Citizens can also work at the polls on election day as **poll workers**—people hired by local election officials to manage the voting—or **poll watchers**—mostly volunteers whom a party or candidate sends to polling places to ensure that the election is running fairly.

Running for office is yet another way citizens can become involved in politics. At the local, state, or national level, many Americans become political candidates in hopes of helping to affect change in their government.

> **How does age affect voter turnout?**
> _____
> _____

## THE VOTING PROCESS

There are three steps to the voting process. First, voters should educate themselves about the candidates, from their experience and background to their stance on major issues.

Second, voters need to register to vote, the process for which can vary from state to state. Some states now allow on-site, election-day registration; others give people the opportunity to register while applying for a driver's license. People are often asked to

> **What should a person know about the candidates before voting?**
> _____
> _____

declare a political party when registering. This is not required information. A person who does not declare a party is simply listed as an independent.

Third, voters need to cast a ballot. The balloting method may involve marking a paper ballot or using a mechanical voting machine.

To ensure that every vote has equal weight, the law requires that every district in a legislative body, federal or state, contains about the same amount of people. Since the population of areas change, the government, by order of the Constitution, conducts a census every 10 years to keep track of these changes. If necessary, seats in the House of Representatives and the state legislatures are reassigned based on census results. This process of drawing new boundaries for legislative districts is called **redistricting**. In instances where state legislatures draw boundaries so that the majority of voters in a district favor one political party over another, the process is called gerrymandering.

Election day is typically one of the busiest days in a campaign. Staff focus their activities around three pieces of information: the places where their candidate has strong support, the places where support for their candidate's opponent is strong, and the places where the voting could go either way. Often avoiding areas where support for an opponent is strong, the candidate and campaign volunteers usually gather near polling places to summon last-minute support. Campaign staff also spends much time and energy on get out the vote, or GOTV, activities. These efforts may consist of phoning voters to ask for their support or offering them a ride to the polls. If poll watchers are allowed at the polls, they alert other staff as to who has not voted yet. Additional GOTV efforts might then be directed at this group of people.

> **Why is redistricting necessary?**
> _____
> _____
> _____

> **What are two ways campaign members try to "get out the vote"?**
> _____
> _____
> _____

# Simulation

Use your Student Casebook to help you complete the simulation.

**Supreme Court Cases**

# Chapter Summary

| First Amendment |
|---|
| • Freedom of expression and assembly |
| • Student speech and school prayer |

| Fourth Amendment |
|---|
| • Unreasonable search and seizure |
| • Expectations of privacy |

**Important Supreme Court Decisions**

| Fourteenth Amendment |
|---|
| • Equal protection under the law |
| • Substantive and procedural due process |

| Commerce Clause |
|---|
| • Doctrine of selective exclusiveness |
| • Questions of regulation |

## COMPREHENSION AND CRITICAL THINKING

Use information from the graphic organizer to answer the following questions.

1. **Describe** What First and Fourth Amendment issues have been influenced by Supreme Court decisions?

_____

2. **Make Inferences** The doctrine of selective exclusiveness identifies when Congress has the power to regulate commerce. Explain why you think this issue would need to be decided by the Supreme Court.

_____

_____

3. **Rate** What is your opinion about the importance of the Fourteenth Amendment? Why do you think "due process" and "equal protection" are essential to Americans?

_____

_____

**Supreme Court Cases**

**READING FOCUS**
Your freedom of expression—the right to practice your religious beliefs; to hold, express, and publish ideas and opinions; to gather with others; and to ask the government to correct its mistakes—is the cornerstone of our democracy. Through its power to interpret the Constitution, the Supreme Court can expand or limit your rights.

## Key Terms

**freedom of expression** the right of citizens to hold, explore, exchange, express, and debate ideas

**redress of grievances** to remove the cause of a complaint and make things right

**right of assembly** the right to form and join groups to gather for any peaceful and lawful purpose

## Taking Notes

As you read the summaries, use your Student Casebook to take notes on the section.

## Case Study Summary

### STUDENTS' RIGHT OF EXPRESSION

In 1965 despite their school's ban on armbands, John and Mary Beth Tinker and other students wore black armbands to school to protest the Vietnam War. When the students were suspended, their families sued the school district, claiming that the teenagers' First Amendment right to free expression had been violated. The district countered that the school had reasonably used its power to preserve order.

The case, *Tinker* v. *Des Moines School District*, was eventually appealed to the Supreme Court. In 1969 the Court reversed the lower courts' rulings, deciding in favor of the students. In the 7–2 majority opinion, justices explained that although schools had the right to maintain order, the expression in question did not substantially interfere with school operation— a standard that has become known as the Tinker test and is still used in free-expression cases involving public-school students. In the decades since the *Tinker* case, though, the Court has ruled against students in cases involving vulgar speech, school-newspaper censorship, and off-campus expression.

> **Explain the Tinker test in your own words.**
> _____
> _____
> _____

# What You Need to Know Summary

## FREEDOM OF RELIGION

**Freedom of expression** is the right of American citizens to hold, explore, exchange, express, and debate ideas. This freedom is guaranteed within the First Amendment. The First Amendment also contains the establishment clause and the free exercise clause when it states that "Congress shall make no law respecting an establishment of religion or the free exercise thereof."

These two clauses have been at the center of many controversial Supreme Court decisions. The establishment clause is most often cited in cases involving the separation of church and state. In 1962 the Court banned a prayer required in public schools, soon following that decision with others that declared certain required prayers and periods of silent meditation illegal—including prayer before school athletic events. The Court has not banned private, voluntary school prayer, however, requiring public schools to allow students to form private religious groups with the stipulation that school employees may not take part. The Court has also ruled that teaching about the religion or the Bible is constitutional, as long as the instruction itself is nonreligious in nature.

While the free exercise clause allows people to believe whatever they want, it does not allow them to *express* their beliefs however they want. The Supreme Court has developed and employs the "compelling interest test," which requires the government to have a compelling reason for banning a religious practice to protect society. This test has been used to decide cases involving polygamy—ruled illegal—and the right to wear religious headwear in the military while on duty—also ruled illegal—as well as many other cases in which the Court declared that what society gained from making a person follow a law was less important that that person's religious freedom.

> **Which part of the Constitution protects freedom of expression?**
> _____

> **What does the free-exercise clause *not* allow people to do?**
> _____

## FREEDOM OF SPEECH

Although the First Amendment states that "Congress shall make no law . . . abridging freedom of speech," the Supreme Court has deemed some speech unprotected over the years, including speech with little or no social value, speech that may inspire violence, speech that defames a person orally (slander) or in print (libel), and speech that is lewd.

Furthermore, the Court has ruled that schools can control the time, place, and content of student expression. The Court and American schools continue to carefully use the Tinker test when considering whether to ban student political speech. The Court has been less open-minded when it comes to vulgar and obscene speech, ruling that it is contrary to a school's mission of teaching socially acceptable behavior. While the Court has not yet ruled on speech codes, it has declared that cyberspeech—speech on the Internet—has the same protections as printed materials. The lower courts have heard several cases involving cyberspeech and have ruled both for and against a school's right to suspend a student for criticizing school officials online.

## FREEDOM OF PETITION AND ASSEMBLY

The freedom of petition—the right to ask the government for a **redress of grievances**, or to remove the cause of a complaint and make things right—and the **right of assembly**, or the right to gather for any peaceful and lawful purpose, are additional guarantees included in the First Amendment. However, the Supreme Court has ruled that the government may sometimes regulate the time, place, and behavior of assemblies on public property, as well as the kinds of groups to which a person may belong.

> When can the government regulate assemblies?
> _____

## STUDENT ASSEMBLY

Freedom of assembly is also sometimes limited in schools. The Supreme Court has ruled that schools have the right to regulate the time, place, and manner of student gatherings; set restrictions on student clubs; and, in some instances, deny students permission to form a new club. Furthermore, the Court holds that schools cannot discriminate against clubs because of their religious or philosophical viewpoints.

# Simulation

Use your Student Casebook to help you complete the simulation.

**Section 2**

### READING FOCUS
The Fourth Amendment guarantees your right to be secure against unreasonable searches and seizures—in other words, it guarantees that you have rights to some forms of privacy. As with First Amendment rights, Fourth Amendment rights are not absolute and are subject to judicial interpretation. In this cyber age, protection of these rights is perhaps more important than ever.

# Key Terms

**search** any action by government to find evidence of criminal activity

**seizure** when authorities keep something found during a search

**plain view doctrine** an assumption under the law that if an object is in plain view, the owner does not consider it private

**Terry stop** when the police stop a person and pat down him or her down for weapons due to the fact that he or she is acting suspiciously and may be a threat to the public interest

**special needs test** standard to determine whether a search serves some safety or security need for society

**cyber-surveillance** searches of wireless communications

**National Security Letter** a document signed, issued and used by the Federal Bureau of Investigation and other agencies to search for information about a person

# Taking Notes

As you read the summaries, use your Student Casebook to take notes on the section.

# Case Study Summary

### THE RIGHT TO PRIVACY

In 1998 Roy Caballes was pulled over by an Illinois state trooper for speeding. While performing a routine check for outstanding warrants, the officer discovered that Caballes had been arrested twice for selling drugs. A nearby officer with a drug-sniffing dog joined the first trooper, and when the dog barked near Caballes's trunk, the officers searched the car, found drugs, and arrested Caballes.

Caballes was convicted and sentenced, but in 2003, the Illinois Supreme Court reversed the conviction, claiming that using the dog at a routine stop was a violation of Caballes's Fourth Amendment rights. The state appealed the ruling to the Supreme Court in *Illinois* v. *Caballes*.

> **Why did the Illinois Supreme Court reverse Caballes's conviction?**
> _____
> _____

In a 6–2 decision issued in 2005, the Court reversed the Illinois Supreme Court's decision and upheld Caballes's conviction, stating that a dog sniff did not constitute a search and that a person has no privacy when in possession of drugs or other contraband. The justices in the majority ruled that because the traffic stop was legal and because the dog had barked as trained to, the state police had enough reasonable suspicion to search Caballes's car.

# What You Need to Know Summary

## UNDERSTANDING SEARCH AND SEIZURE

The Fourth Amendment protects a citizen's rights against unreasonable **searches**—any actions by the government to find evidence of criminal activity—and **seizures**—when authorities keep something. This protection extends only to searches and seizures made by the government, which can include everything from listening in on phone conversations to seizing drugs. A person is seized when his or her movement is restrained by physical force or someone's authority.

The Fourth Amendment also guarantees that warrants—or court orders to search for something or seize someone—can only be obtained if there is probable cause, or good reason, that a search or seizure will produce evidence of a crime or a criminal. In order to prevent what the Constitution calls "unreasonable search and seizure," a warrant must state what authorities are looking for and where. Warrants are not required—although probable cause is—for all searches, seizures, or arrests. For example, the law assumes that if an object is in plain view, its owner does not consider it private and the police therefore do not need a warrant—an assumption called the **plain view doctrine**.

> What is the difference between a search and a seizure?
>
> _____
>
> _____

> Imagine that the police find drugs in a bathroom drawer. Is this an example of the plain-view doctrine? Explain.
>
> _____
>
> _____

## THE FOURTH AMENDMENT AND PRIVACY

A person's right to privacy has limits. The Supreme Court has ruled that a person has an expectation of privacy in certain places, like his or her home and yard, but not in others, such as public places, anywhere when in possession of illegal drugs, or someone else's home.

The privacy a person has over his or her body has also been interpreted in different ways by the Supreme Court. Since the ruling in the 1968 case *Terry* v. *Ohio*, in which the Court decided that police could stop a person who was acting suspiciously and pat them down for weapons, police only need reasonable suspicion for a so-called **Terry stop**. Subsequent rulings have varied as to what authorities can remove from a person's body—and how. In such Fourth Amendment cases, the Court seems to consider a person's legal status, the invasiveness of the search, and whether the search served some safety or security need for society—a standard called the **special needs test**. DNA, blood, and urine tests are typically considered intrusive, although the Court has ruled that it is legal to conduct random drugs tests on some public-safety workers and students involved in extra-curricular activities. Public-school students—and sometimes their lockers—can also be searched by school officials if the circumstances behind the search are reasonable.

> **What issues does the Supreme Court consider when deciding if a search of a person's body was legal?**
>
> _____
>
> _____

Recent technology has made it necessary to apply the Fourth Amendment in new ways. The Supreme Court has yet to hear a case involving **cyber-surveillance**, or searches of wireless communications. Currently, authorities must obtain a warrant to intercept wireless communications, although the 2001 USA PATRIOT Act relaxed the process for getting warrants, as well as searches and seizures. The PATRIOT Act makes it possible for the Federal Bureau of Investigation and other government agencies to issue and use a document called a **National Security Letter** (NSL), instead of a warrant granted by a judge, to require almost anyone to turn over consumer records and other information. Authorities do not need probable cause to get a NSL. Given these new developments, the Supreme Court is likely to hear several cases challenging government surveillance programs currently in the federal courts, a task that will involve balancing citizens' Fourth Amendment rights with the government's responsibility for national security.

> **Who issues a National Security Letter?**
>
> _____

# Simulation

Use your Student Casebook to help you complete the simulation.

**Supreme Court Cases**

**READING FOCUS**
The Fourteenth Amendment requires that states provide due process and equal protection under the law. These requirements have made this amendment one of the most important parts of the Constitution.

## Key Terms

**unenumerated rights** those rights that are not explicitly stated in the Constitution

## Taking Notes

As you read the summaries, use your Student Casebook to take notes on the section.

## Case Study Summary

### DUE PROCESS AND PUBLIC SCHOOLS

In 1971 a Columbus, Ohio, high school suspended several students for misconduct. One of the students, Dwight Lopez, claimed he had been an innocent bystander and filed a lawsuit—with several other students as additional plaintiffs—that claimed he should have been entitled to a hearing. When a district court ruled that due process had been denied, the school system appealed to the Supreme Court.

In *Goss* v. *Lopez*, school official Norval Goss argued that Ohio students did not have a constitutional right to public education and therefore no expectation of due process. The students' lawyers countered that Ohio law requires the state to provide free education and that a lack of due process potentially deprived students of this education. The Supreme Court sided with the students, ruling that before or shortly after a suspension, students must be allowed a hearing—although they are not allowed to call or cross-examine witnesses.

> **Why did Lopez claim his right to due process was violated?**
>
> _____
>
> _____

## What You Need to Know Summary

### DUE PROCESS AND EQUAL PROTECTION

The Fourteenth Amendment declares that no state will deprive a person of "life, liberty, or property, without due process of law," nor deny a person "equal protection of laws"—including against actions of the federal government. The due-process clause means that laws and the processes and procedures for applying and enforcing laws must be fair—known as substantive due process and procedural due process, respectively. The equal opportunity clause means that the law must be applied the same way to every person.

> **How does the equal-opportunity clause protect Americans?**
>
> _____
>
> _____

## SUBSTANTIVE DUE PROCESS

The Ninth Amendment has been interpreted to protect rights that are not explicitly stated, known as **unenumerated rights**. Through the doctrine of substantive due process, the Supreme Court has recognized some of these rights.

In the landmark 1896 case *Lochner* v. *New York*, the Supreme Court addressed property rights. Bakery owner Joseph Lochner was arrested for requiring an employee to work more than 60 hours a week—a situation illegal in bakeries under New York law. Lochner appealed his conviction to the Supreme Court, arguing that since the New York law applied only to bakery workers, it violated the equal-protection clause. He also argued that the law violated the due-process clause, since it deprived him of his property rights—here, the right to negotiate an employment contract—without due process. The Supreme Court agreed with Lochner, ruling 5–4 that New York's public-health regulation was not truly reasonable or necessary and interfered with the rights of.employers and employees to make contracts.

Backlash over *Lochner* and later Supreme Court property-rights cases prompted the Court to announce in 1938 that it would apply only a rational basis test for economic regulations going forward. For the Court to uphold a law, the government would only have to show that the law had a rational basis.

> **According to the Supreme Court's ruling in *Lochner*, how did the New York law violate residents' property rights?**
>
> _____
>
> _____

After 1938 the Court used substantive due process to define personal unenumerated rights, including the privacy right to die in the 1990 case *Cruzan* v. *Director, Missouri State Department of Health*. Missouri resident Nancy Beth Cruzan was seriously injured in a car accident in 1983. After Cruzan spent years unconscious, her parents asked the hospital to remove her feeding tube and allow her to die. When the hospital refused, Cruzan's parents successfully sued, but the Missouri Supreme Court overturned the ruling. The U.S. Supreme Court upheld the lower court of appeals ruling, noting that although the privacy right to refuse medical treatment was protected under the Fourteenth Amendment, the lack of evidence that ending life support was what Cruzan wanted violated her right to due process.

## PROCEDURAL DUE PROCESS

Two landmark cases established minimum standards for procedural due process in cases involving property rights. In the 1970 case *Goldberg* v. *Kelly*, the Supreme Court declared government payments a kind of property, of which a person cannot be denied or have terminated without due process of law, such as a hearing. In the 1972 case *Stanley* v. *Illinois*, the court ruled that unwed fathers are entitled to due process hearings to determine their fitness as a parent before their children can be taken away, a decision that established that every American is entitled to at least a formal notice and hearing before the government can deprive him or her of rights or property.

> Why was the Court's decision in *Stanley* v. *Illinois* important to all Americans?
> _____
> _____

The Supreme Court has also clearly defined procedural due process in cases involving juveniles, particularly in the case *In re Gault*. This case involved Arizona teenager Gerald Gault, who, after being accused of making an obscene phone call, was found guilty and sentenced to six years in a state industrial school. Gault was not advised he could have an attorney, his family did not testify, no one testified under oath, no record was made of the hearing, and Gault was not given his Sixth Amendment right to confront his accuser.

Since Gault did not have the right to appeal under Arizona law, his parents petitioned the Supreme Court for his release. In a 8–1 decision in favor of the petitioners, the Court declared that the Fourteenth Amendment applied to minors and adults alike. This ruling gave juveniles almost all of the same due process rights as adult defendants.

> Name two ways Gault's Fourteenth Amendment rights were violated.
> _____
> _____

# Simulation

Use your Student Casebook to help you complete the simulation.

**Supreme Court Cases**

**READING FOCUS**
In Chapter 4 you read that federalism is a system of government in which power is divided between a central government and regional governments. The Constitution gives the national government power over some issues and reserves to the state governments power over other issues. The balance of power between the national government and states shifts from time to time as a result of legislation and Supreme Court decisions.

## Key Terms

**selective exclusiveness** a doctrine that states that only Congress may regulate commerce that requires national, uniform regulation

## Taking Notes

As you read the summaries, use your Student Casebook to take notes on the section.

## Case Study Summary

### TREATIES AND STATES' RIGHTS

In 1916 the United States and Great Britain signed a treaty to protect birds that migrated between the United States and Canada. Two years later Congress passed the Migratory Bird Treaty Act to implement the treaty and make it illegal to kill or capture any bird mentioned in the treaty. Missouri state officials tried to prevent federal game warden Ray Holland from enforcing the act, claiming that it was an unconstitutional use of federal power. A federal district court disagreed. Missouri then appealed the decision to the Supreme Court.

In *Missouri* v. *Holland* federal attorneys argued that the Constitution gives the president the power to make treaties and also, through the supremacy clause, makes the Constitution, treaties, and federal laws the supreme law of the land. Missouri's attorneys argued that Congress had passed legislation that violated the Tenth Amendment and intruded upon Missouri's sovereign powers. They also argued that Congress should not be able to use the president's treaty power to pass a law that would otherwise be unconstitutional.

In 1920 the Supreme Court upheld the lower court's decision, stating that the supremacy clause

> **What made it possible for Congress to pass the Migratory Bird Treaty Act?**
>
> _____
>
> _____

gives Congress the right to implement treaties, including regulating activities within states.

# What You Need to Know Summary

## EXPANDING FEDERAL AUTHORITY

Article I, Section 8, Clause 3 of the Constitution, known as the commerce clause, states that Congress has the right "to regulate commerce with foreign nations, and among the several states, and with the Indian tribes." Over the years, the way Congress has used and the Supreme Court has interpreted this clause has defined the U.S. system of federalism. For example, Congress used its right to control commerce between states—known as interstate commerce—to help end racial discrimination—with the help of the Supreme Court. In 1964 the Court ruled that part of the recently passed Civil Rights Act of 1964 could be applied to private businesses—such as motels with guests from several states—to force them from discriminating against African Americans.

> **How does the commerce clause help define federalism?**
> _____
> _____

## THE COMMERCE CLAUSE AND THE COURT

Until the mid-1800s, Congress hardly ever employed the commerce clause to expand federal power. But in 1852, in *Cooley* v. *Board Warden*, the Supreme Court established the doctrine of **selective exclusiveness**, which states that when commerce requires national, uniform regulation, only Congress may regulate it. Otherwise states may regulate it.

After *Cooley*, Congress became more secure in regulating commerce that fell under its jurisdiction. However, as *United States* v. *Lopez* and *Gonzales* v. *Raich* show, selective exclusiveness is not always applied exactly the same way by the Supreme Court.

In 1992 San Antonio, Texas teenager Alfonso Lopez brought a gun to school. Once questioned by school officials, Lopez admitted he had a gun and was arrested under Texas law with firearm possession on school property. The next day all state charges were dropped so that federal officials could charge Lopez with violating Section 922(q) of the federal Gun-Free School Zones Act of 1990. Lopez was convicted and sentenced in federal court, but the conviction was reversed upon appeal. Federal officials appealed this

> **According to the doctrine of selective exclusiveness, when can states regulate commerce?**
> _____
> _____

reversal to the Supreme Court in *United States* v.
*Lopez*, arguing that guns in school zones could lead to
violent crime and interrupt students' learning, both
outcomes that could affect the economy and therefore
were Congress's responsibility to regulate under the
commerce clause. Lopez's lawyers argued that having
a gun in school was a criminal offense but had nothing
to do with interstate commerce. In a 5–4 decision, the
Supreme Court agreed with Lopez and declared the
Gun-Free School Zones Act unconstitutional. This
was the first time Congress's use of the commerce
clause had been limited since the 1930s.

    The Supreme Court again debated Congress's use
of the commerce clause in the 2005 case *Gonzales* v.
*Reich*. In 1996 California voters approved the use of
marijuana, illegal under federal law, for medical
purposes. Two California residents, Diane Monson
and Angel Raich, began growing marijuana at home to
relieve chronic pain. In 2002, federal authorities
seized their plants, prompting Monson and Raich to
successfully sue the federal government.

    After the court of appeals also ruled in the
plaintiffs' favor, the government appealed to the
Supreme Court. Monson and Raich's lawyers argued
that the federal law allowing the seizure overstepped
Congress's power to regulate interstate commerce,
since everything used to grow the plants was from
California. Federal lawyers countered that, through
the supremacy clause, federal law took precedence
over state law. They also argued that homegrown
marijuana could affect the illegal trade in marijuana
coming into California from other states and
countries, therefore giving the federal government the
right to regulate it.

    In a 6–3 decision—and in spite of a strong dissent
saying that the principles of federalism should protect
California's actions—the Supreme Court agreed with
the federal government that marijuana, although
illegal, is a part of commerce and that the commerce
clause therefore applied to the situation.

> **Why did the federal government believe that guns in school zones should be regulated by Congress?**
>
> _____
>
> _____

> **How was the Court's decision in *Gonzales* v. *Raich* different than in *United States* v. *Lopez*?**
>
> _____
>
> _____

# Simulation

Use your Student Casebook to help you complete the simulation.

**Making Foreign Policy**

# Chapter Summary

| U.S. Foreign Policy | |
|---|---|
| Goals | Protect national security, establish free and open trade, promote world peace, support democracy, and provide aid to people in need |
| Influences | President, Congress, Departments of State and Defense, CIA, interest groups, public opinion, media |
| Past and Present | Transition from isolationism to important role in international politics, supporting developing democracies and global foreign-aid efforts |
| Role in United Nations | Help to maintain international peace and security, develop friendly relations among nations, and achieve international cooperation |

## COMPREHENSION AND CRITICAL THINKING

Use information from the graphic organizer to answer the following questions.

1. **Recall** What are the primary goals of U.S. foreign policy?

_____

_____

2. **Analyze** Why do you think international cooperation is a key UN goal?

_____

_____

3. **Predict** How might public opinion contribute to foreign policy decisions?

_____

_____

## Making Foreign Policy

> **READING FOCUS**
> Foreign policy is a nation's plans and procedures for dealing with other countries.
> Although U.S. foreign policy has changed over time, it has been guided by five
> basic goals and formulated through a set of theories, tools, and strategies.

## Key Terms

**foreign policy** a nation's set of plans and procedures for dealing with foreign countries

**isolationism** an approach to foreign policy in which a government's leaders look after
domestic issues and stay out of world affairs in order to avoid war

**internationalist** an approach to foreign policy in which a country takes an active role in
international politics as the best way to pursue national security

**embassies** diplomatic centers

**defense alliance** an agreement between nations to come to each other's aid in the event
of an attack

**collective security** attempts at keeping international peace and order

**economic sanctions** acts of withholding money

**just war theory** a theory of warfare in which a state may justly got o war under certain
specific circumstances and must limit its conduct according to certain standards

## Taking Notes

As you read the summaries, use your Student Casebook to take notes on
the section.

## Case Study Summary

### GENOCIDE IN RWANDA

Once Rwanda gained its independence from Belgium
in 1962, the Hutus, the largest ethnic group, took
control of the government, killing or exiling thousands
of Tutus, the chief minority. By 1990 a Tutsi rebel
group had formed, and after an unsuccessful attempt
to overthrow the Hutus, began talks with Hutu leader
Juvénal Habyarimana. After Habyarimana died in a
plane crash in 1994, however, the country slipped into
chaos. Hutu extremists killed both moderate members
of their own group and 800,000 Tutsi people and
sympathizers.

> Who controlled the
> Rwandan government once
> the country gained
> independence?
>
> _____
> _____

Despite the fact that it had signed a United Nations
convention to prevent genocide, the United States and
President Bill Clinton decided only to issue a

statement of shock and sadness about the Rwanda killings, instead of intervening. The United States had recently lost U.S. forces during a peacekeeping mission in Somalia and was reluctant to repeat that tragedy. In July 1994, President Clinton sent 200 troops to Rwanda for humanitarian relief, but the genocide was already over.

# What You Need to Know Summary
## THE BASICS OF FOREIGN POLICY

The **foreign policy** of the United States is its plans and procedures for dealing with foreign countries. Although it varies from president to president, foreign policy ultimately has five goals: protect national security, establish free and open trade, promote world peace, support democracy in the interest of stability and open markets, and provide aid to people in need.

There are many theories as to how the United States should approach foreign policy. Up until World War I, the U.S. government followed a policy of **isolationism**, mostly staying out of world affairs in order to avoid war. Since then, however, the country has been heavily involved in international politics. Americans who consider themselves realists prefer the **internationalist** approach, which promotes international cooperation, such as alliances, to protect national security. Others believe neoisolationism is the best course of action, by which the United States refrains from most involvement in foreign affairs in the interest of itself and other countries. Finally, idealists are split on the idea of military action but firmly believe in foreign policy as a method for promoting democracy and supporting human rights.

> How is the internationalist approach to foreign policy different than the isolationist approach?
>
> _____
> _____
> _____
> _____

## THE TOOLS OF FOREIGN POLICY

Besides persuasion and power, the United States relies on diplomatic, economic, and military tools to accomplish its foreign policy.

Diplomacy helps the country protect itself by maintaining healthy relationships with other nations. The United States has more than 160 **embassies**, or diplomatic centers, around the world. American presidents have also signed treaties with leaders all over the globe. Additionally, the country belongs to

> Why is diplomacy so important?
>
> _____
> _____
> _____

Section 1 *continued*

**defensive alliances**. All nations within an alliance agree to come to each other's aid in the event of an attack. This is an example of **collective security**, or attempts at keeping international peace and order.

Economic foreign-policy tools include foreign aid and sanctions. By offering nonmilitary aid to countries in need through the United States Agency for International Development (USAID), the United States helps spread democracy and expands free markets. Military aid is also sometimes provided to other nations' armed forces. **Economic sanctions** occur when a country or countries withhold money—by restricting imports, exports, trade, or financial transactions—to pressure another nation to make social or political changes.

Using military force within another nation is an extremely important decision. Although Congress is the governmental body with the power to declare war, it has primarily been the president who has initiated most American military action. When considering such action, the president may listen to several advisers, including the secretary of state, the secretary of defense, the Joint Chiefs of Staff, and members of the Central Intelligence Agency and the National Security Council.

| What is the purpose of economic sanctions? |
| --- |
| _____ |
| _____ |
| _____ |

## JUST WAR THEORY

According to the **just war theory**, a state may justly—or fairly—go to war under certain specific circumstances and must limit its conduct according to certain standards. War theorists call the justification of a war *jus ad bellum* and how to conduct it *jus in bello*. *Jud as bellum* is defined by four principles: a state must openly declare war and have a just cause for doing so; justice must be the purpose of the war; the state must have considered all costs and benefits of warfare and any other possible resolutions before declaring war; and the war's only goal must be an outcome of just peace. *Jus in bello* limits the conduct of war to military targets only and forbids any action beyond what is necessary to achieve the war's goal.

| According to the just war theory, what should the only goal of war be? |
| --- |
| _____ |

# Simulation

Use your Student Casebook to help you complete the simulation.

# Making Foreign Policy

**READING FOCUS**
U.S. foreign policy is directed and shaped by the executive branch and Congress and is carried out by a large bureaucracy. Domestic influences such as interest groups also play a role in foreign policy.

## Key Terms

**foreign service** the approximately 20,000 State Department employees who work overseas

**presidential doctrines** foreign policy statements that guide the direction of U.S. foreign policy

**diplomatic recognition** the act of acknowledging a government as the proper representative of its country's people

## Taking Notes

As you read the summaries, use your Student Casebook to take notes on the section.

## Case Study Summary

### ELIÁN GONZÁLEZ

In November 1999, two American fishermen discovered a six-year-old Cuban boy named Elián González floating off the coast of Florida. The refugee boat he had been on with his mother and stepfather had capsized and he was one of only three survivors. Elián was placed with Cuban-American relatives in Miami, who wished for him to remain in the United States. However, back in Cuba, Elián's father and Cuban president Fidel Castro demanded that he be returned.

For many Cuban Americans, Elián became a symbol in their struggle with Fidel Castro, against whose communist government they wished to place an embargo. Elián's Miami family made several attempts to keep him in the United States, yet the fact remained that he had entered the country illegally. In early 2000, the U.S. Immigration and Naturalization Service (ISN) announced that Elián's father was responsible for his custody. The Department of State then allowed Elián's father to come to the United States, where the U.S. Attorney General met with him. Yet the Miami relatives did not agree to release Elián to his father.

> **What did Elián González come to symbolize for some Cuban Americans?**
> _____
> _____
> _____

INS agents finally stormed the home where Elián was
being held, removed him, and returned him to his
father. Protests broke out in Miami, and Elián's
American relatives appealed to the Supreme Court.
The Court rejected the case only hours before Elián
and his father returned to Cuba.

# What You Need to Know Summary
## THE FOREIGN POLICY BUREAUCRACY

There are many players involved in the U.S. foreign-
policy bureaucracy, the administrative structure that
carries out U.S. foreign policy on a day-to-day basis.

The most important foreign-policy agency is the
Department of State, which manages all international
relations and diplomatic efforts within the executive
departments. Many of the department's bureaus and
agencies are outside the United States. In fact, about
13,700 employees from the Department of State work
overseas in what is known as the **foreign service**.
These employees carry out foreign policy abroad and
relay information about other countries to U.S.
policymakers.

> Who makes up the foreign service?
> _____
> _____

The Department of Defense supervises U.S.
military actions and advises the president on related
issues. Included within the department are its head,
the secretary of defense, and the Joint Chiefs of
Staff—the leaders of every branch of the military.

The Central Intelligence Agency (CIA) is the third
major player in U.S. foreign policy. Through both
transparent and covert activities, the CIA collects and
analyzes information about other nations.

> Explain the purpose of the Central Intelligence Agency.
> _____
> _____
> _____

At times, foreign policy can also be affected by
domestic influences. While creating legislation
concerning foreign policy, policymakers may feel
pressured by constituents and by their own political
party. Lobbyists can also influence policymakers.

## THE PRESIDENT, CONGRESS, AND FOREIGN POLICY

As the country's ambassador to the world, the
president regularly spends time building international
relationships that benefit American security and the
economy. The Constitution grants the president the
power to negotiate treaties, which are later ratified by

Congress; issue **presidential doctrines**, or foreign policy statements that guide foreign policy; make executive, or informal, agreements with the heads of other nations; and decide whether to grant a nation **diplomatic recognition**, or an official acknowledgement by the United States that a government is the proper representative of its people.

As commander in chief, the president also has the power to initiate military action against and within foreign nations—such as short-term military strikes—even without a declaration of war issued by Congress. Since the passage of the War Powers Act in 1973, however, presidents have been limited in how they can take independent action. If a president commits troops, he or she now must work closely with Congress to determine further action.

In terms of foreign policy, the Constitution grants Congress the power to declare war, appropriate or deny funds, ratify treaties, and confirm presidential appointments. Congress can also initiate foreign policy by introducing resolutions, establishing programs, setting guidelines, directing the executive branch, and making funding requests. Policymakers can also give advice and use legislation and funding restrictions to support or change the president's foreign-policy actions. Additionally, Congress holds oversight hearings and investigations on how well executive agencies are carrying out foreign policy.

> Why are more limits placed on how presidents authorize military activity today than there were 50 years ago?
>
> _____
> _____
> _____
> _____

## INTEREST GROUPS AND FOREIGN POLICY

Interest groups are another force that can affect the way policymakers approach foreign policy. These groups provide specialized information to both policymakers and the public in hopes of influencing relevant legislation. Similarly, public opinion and the ways in which public opinion is shaped by various media outlets can have an impact on foreign-policy decisions-making.

> Why do interest groups attempt to educate policymakers?
>
> _____
> _____

# Simulation

Use your Student Casebook to help you complete the simulation.

## Making Foreign Policy

**Section 3**

**READING FOCUS**
The United States is a member of international organizations that work to maintain peace and political stability around the world.

## Key Terms

**UN Security Council** a 15-member division of the United Nations that is charged with maintaining international peace and security

**trust territory** a colony or territory placed under administration by another country or countries

## Taking Notes

As you read the summaries, use your Student Casebook to take notes on the section.

## Case Study Summary

### MAKING THE CASE FOR WAR

In 1990 a U.S.-led coalition attacked Iraq in response to the country's invasion of Kuwait. The United Nations (UN) authorized the attacks, and at the cease-fire, required Iraq to stop developing nuclear weapons.

In October 2002, Congress voted to authorize President George W. Bush to use force in Iraq if it was proven that Iraq had violated the UN requirement. Although the UN warned Iraq to fully disarm and continued its weapons inspections, the international organization did not agree to pass a resolution to attack Iraq.

President Bush decided to attack without formally asking the UN Security Council to issue a resolution authorizing military action, and without asking for the help of other member nations. Some international critics claimed this decision should not have been made by the United States alone and that it marginalized the value and efforts of international organizations like the United Nations.

> Why did some critics believe President Bush's actions marginalized the United Nations?
>
> _____
> _____
> _____
> _____

## What You Need to Know Summary

### THE UNITED NATIONS

The United Nations (UN) was established in 1945, at the end of World War II, as a replacement for the

League of Nations. It includes 192 member nations. The UN's charter breaks the organization's purpose into four goals: maintain international peace and security; develop friendly relations among nations based on respect for equal rights and the self-determination of peoples; achieve international cooperation in solving economic, social, cultural, and humanitarian problems; and be a center for harmonizing how members' actions attain these common goals.

There are six major divisions in the UN, within which are dozens of smaller agencies. First, all states meet as the General Assembly to discuss and vote on what to do about important international matters. Critical matters require a two-thirds majority, but less critical votes need only a simple majority. All votes and their consequences are advisory, not binding.

Second, 15 member nations form the **UN Security Council**. These members are responsible for maintaining international peace and security, and the decisions they make—a supermajority, or nine votes, is required—do hold authority. Such decisions may include economic sanctions or collective military action. There are 10 elected member nations and five permanent member nations: China, France, the Russian Federation, the United Kingdom, and the United States.

The third division of the UN is the Economic and Social Council (ECOSOC), which coordinates dozens of UN organizations and thousands of nongovernmental organizations (NGOs) that work to increase living standards in developing countries and universal respect for human rights.

The International Court of Justice (ICJ), or World Court, is the fourth UN division. Fifteen judges elected by the General Assembly and Security Council hear cases voluntarily presented by both member and nonmember states, then issue final, binding verdicts based on international law.

The fifth division is the Trusteeship Council. Tasked with administering the UN **trust territories**—colonies or territories placed under administration by another country or countries—the Council now only

> **Summarize the purpose of the United Nations in your own words.**
> _____
> _____
> _____
> _____
> _____

> **How are votes by the Security Council different than those by the General Assembly?**
> _____
> _____
> _____

meets on an as-needed basis, since all former trust territories are now independent.

Finally, the Secretariat is the sixth UN division. This group is responsible for the administration and coordination of UN efforts. Staff members are considered part of an international civil service and only take orders from the UN. The Secretariat is headed by the Secretary General, who is elected every five years—with the chance of reelection—by the General Assembly, on the recommendation of the Security Council. The Secretary-General is a very public figure and acts as the chief administrative officer at meetings held by all other UN divisions except the ICJ.

> **Name the six main divisions of the United Nations.**
>
> _____
>
> _____
>
> _____
>
> _____
>
> _____

## OTHER INTERNATIONAL INSTITUTIONS

Large organizations affiliated with the United Nations govern the world's economic and judicial systems. The World Trade Organization's (WTO) 162 members make up about 97 percent of world trade. The WTO works to ensure equal-access trade among countries. The International Monetary Fund (IMF) includes almost all world nations and mainly loans money to less-developed countries whose economies are stuck in debt. Similarly, the World Bank works to assist developing nations meet specific goals, such as road construction or additional funding for agriculture.

> **Who do the International Monetary Fund and the World Bank try to help?**
>
> _____
>
> _____

In addition to the UN's World Court, the International Criminal Court (ICC) and international tribunals act as world judicial organizations. The ICC, established in 2002, is considered "a court of last resort" and hears cases that UN member nations cannot or will not prosecute, as well as cases referred by the UN Security Council. The ICC is treaty-based and prosecutes individuals accused of genocide, war crimes, and crimes against humanity. International tribunals were formed before the existence of the ICC to prosecute specific atrocities in Yugoslavia and Rwanda and will expire when their work is complete.

# Simulation

Use your Student Casebook to help you complete the simulation.

## Making Foreign Policy

**Section 4**

### READING FOCUS
Helping countries make the transition to democracy and overcome poverty are some foreign policy challenges facing the United States.

## Key Terms

**Monroe Doctrine** a foreign-policy statement issued in 1823 in which the United States proclaimed its intention to remain neutral during European conflicts

**deterrence** a policy of building up the U.S. armed forces in order to discourage acts of military aggression by other nations

**containment** a policy based on the view that communism threatened democratic values and that Soviet expansion must be stopped

**détente** a relaxing of tensions

**preemptive strike** the potential use of force before an attack occurs

**democratization** the establishment of democratic governments

**food security** an adequate food supply at the national, household, and individual level

## Taking Notes

As you read the summaries, use your Student Casebook to take notes on the section.

## Case Study Summary

### THE CZECH REPUBLIC

Still a young nation at the end of World War II, Czechoslovakia fell under Communist control by 1948, ending its history as the only democracy in Eastern Europe. By the 1960s, the Soviet-style Czech economy was in crisis. Attempts by a reform movement within the country's Communist party to initiate economic and democratic reforms were quickly squelched by Soviet troops.

One of the loudest voices to speak out against Czechoslovakia's communist government belonged to Václav Havel. Havel became a leader in the 1970s and 1980s human-rights movement, demanding with other dissidents that citizens be granted the civil and political rights to which they were entitled. He also started the hugely popular Civic Reform, an antigovernment coalition of reform groups.

> **What did Václav Havel wish for his people?**
>
> _____
> _____
> _____

By 1989 huge demonstrations led to the collapse of
the country's communist government, a mostly
nonviolent event now called the Velvet Revolution.
Havel was elected interim president. In 1993 the
Czech and Slovak republics peacefully separated and
became independent states.

# What You Need to Know Summary

## PAST FOREIGN POLICY CHANGES

For several decades after the United States won its
independence, the country mostly maintained a policy
of isolationism and neutrality. In 1823 the government
issued the **Monroe Doctrine** to proclaim America's
intentions to remain neutral during European conflicts.
U.S. foreign policy followed this doctrine until the
late 1800s, when the country began to shift to more of
an internationalist policy, best seen by its role in the
Spanish-American War of 1898, from which the
United States emerged a world power. After German
attacks on U.S. ships, the country also entered World
War I in 1917. Resentment over the brutality of World
War I kept the country from participating in World
War II until Japanese planes attacked Hawaii in 1941,
at which point Congress declared war.

After World War II, U.S. foreign policy began to
center around collective security—working with other
nations to keep international peace and order—and
**deterrence**, the policy of building up the U.S. armed
forces to discourage acts of military aggression by
other nations. Deterrence was in large part directed at
the Soviet Union, which began taking control of
Eastern Europe after World War II. Determined to
stop the spread of communism, which reached Asia by
1949, the United States also began following a policy
of **containment**, which was based on the view that
communism threatened democratic values and that
Soviet expansion must be stopped.

As part of this policy, the United States became
involved in two undeclared wars, the Korean War and
the Vietnam War, during the 1950s, 1960s, and 1970s.
The country was also briefly involved with
Communist Cuba in 1962, eventually persuading the
Soviet Union to remove nuclear missiles it had been
planning to place there.

> Describe U.S. foreign
> policy up until the late
> 1800s.
>
> _____
>
> _____
>
> _____

> What did the United States
> hope to achieve by
> following a policy of
> containment?
>
> _____
>
> _____
>
> _____
>
> _____

The Soviet Union began to collapse from within by the late 1980s. This followed a period of U.S.-Soviet **détente**, or a relaxing of tensions. By the early 1990s, the tension between the two countries, long known as the Cold War, had largely disappeared.

## CONTEMPORARY FOREIGN POLICY CHANGES

Although the Cold War is over, the United States still faces many foreign-policy challenges, including how to stop the spread of nuclear weapons. U.S. leaders also struggle to maintain relationships with oil-rich but typically non-democratic countries in the Middle East. The U.S.-Israel alliance bothers many Muslims in the region. The U.S. invasions of Afghanistan and Iraq following the September 11, 2001, terrorist attacks are another point of contention, although the United States considers both actions part of a **preemptive strike** doctrine, or the potential use of force before an attack occurs.

> **What factors currently strain the relationship between the United Sates and some Middle Eastern nations?**
>
> _____
> _____
> _____
> _____

Current U.S. foreign policy also includes support of **democratization**, or the establishment of democratic governments. The United States works on supporting the economies of the former Soviet republics; the struggling democracies that replaced dictatorships in some Latin America countries; the shaky democratic governments of Afghanistan and Iraq, both affected by political and religious sects; and transitional African democracies, many of which still need to firmly establish the idea of the rule of law.

Giving foreign aid to overcome poverty remains a huge part of U.S. foreign policy. Current efforts include working with other nations to promote **food security**, or an adequate food supply at the national, household, and individual level, in poor regions of the globe. The United States also runs literacy programs around the world, including some that specifically promote gender equality in education. Additionally, the United States is part of several international organizations intent on eradicating the three deadly diseases of malaria, tuberculosis, and HIV/AIDS.

> **Name two goals of U.S. foreign aid.**
>
> _____
> _____
> _____
> _____

# Simulation

Use your Student Casebook to help you complete the simulation.

# Comparative Political and Economic Systems

## Chapter Summary

| System | Characteristics |
|---|---|
| Democratic government | social welfare policies, protection of human rights, stable structure |
| Authoritarian government | disregard for civil and human rights, unequal power concentration |
| Traditional economy | economic choices made according to custom |
| Market economy | economic choices made by individuals and businesses |
| Command economy | economic choices made by the government |
| Mixed economy | elements of traditional, market, and command economies |

## COMPREHENSION AND CRITICAL THINKING

Use information from the graphic organizer to answer the following questions.

1. **Define** What is a mixed economy?

_____

_____

2. **Make Generalizations** What adjectives could you use to describe democratic governments?

_____

_____

3. **Predict** Why does it make sense that civil and human rights are considered unimportant in a government where power is unevenly distributed?

_____

_____

_____

## Comparative Political and Economic Systems

**READING FOCUS**
Today many of the world's countries are democracies. Democracies consist of two basic forms of government: presidential and parliamentary. All democratic governments share certain characteristics, but no two governments are exactly alike.

# Key Terms

**authoritarian** a type of government in which power is concentrated in the hands of a single leader or small group

**coalition** a temporary alliance for political purposes

**apartheid** a system of racial segregation and oppression in place in South African before the 1990s

# Taking Notes

As you read the summaries, use your Student Casebook to take notes on the section.

# Case Study Summary

## EMERGING DEMOCRACY IN NIGERIA

After years as a British colony, Nigeria gained independence in 1960. Its first government, a parliamentary system, suffered many setbacks, ranging from a bloody civil war between different regional, ethnic, and religious groups to dictatorships and assassinations. In the 1970s, Nigeria switched its government to a form more closely resembling that of the United States, establishing three independent branches of government and allowing for the popular election of the president.

Yet for years the country continued to lack a stable government, and a series of takeovers and fraudulent elections ensued. However, the election of General Olusegan Obasanjo—a former military ruler who became a reform and human rights leader—in the late 1990s and the first peaceful presidential election in 2007 have both been signs of Nigeria's gradual political stability. After years of dishonest government, the country's leaders will now need to work diligently to earn the people's trust and ensure free, open, and fair elections.

> What challenges do Nigeria's leaders face today?
>
> _____
> _____
> _____

# What You Need to Know Summary

## DEMOCRATIC SYSTEMS

Governments are categorized by who holds power and how it is distributed. In a democracy, much power rests with the voters and the leaders they elect, whereas in an **authoritarian** government, power is concentrated in the hands of one ruler or small group. Today nearly half of the countries in the world are democracies. While the power of the head of state can vary, all democracies include social welfare policies, protection of basic human rights, and the ability to withstand national crises without changing structure.

## MEXICO AND BRAZIL

Like the United States, both Mexico and Brazil are democracies with a presidential form of government, three branches, and a federal system. In Mexico, three-fifths of the seats in the bicameral legislature are elected, with the rest distributed in proportion to parties' share of the popular vote. The president is directly elected and the judicial branch is independent. For many years, the Institutional Revolutionary Party (PRI) held power, but recently the National Action Party (PAN) has taken control of the presidency. Although the country has a fairly stable economy, Mexico's government faces many challenges, including modernization and job growth.

| How are members of Mexico's legislature chosen? |
| --- |
| _____ |
| _____ |

After years of political upheaval, Brazil enacted a revised constitution in 1985. The elected legislature is made up of a senate and a chamber of deputies, and the president and vice president are also directly elected. The judicial branch consists of three levels. Voting is mandatory for people between 18 and 70. Brazil's four major parties make it necessary for politicians to work together to achieve goals.

## THE UNITED KINGDOM AND JAPAN

The United Kingdom and Japan are both examples of the world's most common form of democracy, the parliamentary system. In this system, the legislature is the most powerful branch and is responsible for choosing—and possibly removing—the chief executive, known as the prime minister or premier.

| What control does the legislature have over the executive branch in a parliamentary system? |
| --- |
| _____ |
| _____ |

Over the centuries, the United Kingdom has developed into a constitutional monarchy—the hereditary monarch is largely ceremonial—with a unitary government; local governments have only as much power as the central government gives them. The legislature, Parliament, is made up of the elected House of Commons and the limited House of Lords, where members are chosen by political parties or inheritance. Given the number of parties in Parliament, politicians often must set aside their differences and form **coalitions**, or temporary alliances made for political purposes. The prime minister is the leader of the majority party in Parliament and the nation's head of state.

After World War II and with the help of the United States, Japan enacted a democratic constitution in 1947. Japan's unitary system of government is similar to that of the United Kingdom. A bicameral legislature called the Diet is mostly elected, although some seats are distributed based on a party's share of the popular vote. The prime minister is the head of government and the emperor is the head of state.

> **Why do politicians in Parliament need to form coalitions?**
> _____
> _____

## EMERGING DEMOCRACIES

Young democracies face many challenges as they develop. In Latin America, several nations are struggling to establish constitutional democracies while overcoming a long history of authoritarian leadership. Similarly, in Africa, where authoritarian governments were common after countries achieved independence in the years following World War II, democracies are still developing. The country of South Africa, after years of **apartheid**—a system of racial segregation and oppression—successfully established a democracy in 1994 with the election of Nelson Mandela, the country's first black president. In Asia, the change from colony to democracy has also been gradual and sometimes bloody, as countries such as Cambodia have endured civil war and other serious roadblocks on the path to democracy.

> **Why do you think South Africa might be a symbol of hope for other African nations?**
> _____
> _____

# Simulation

Use your Student Casebook to help you complete the simulation.

## Comparative Political and Economic Systems

**Section 2**

 **READING FOCUS**
Democracy has spread throughout the world in recent decades, but some
countries are still under the rule of authoritarian governments. Citizens in these
countries have little control over their own government and, in some cases, over
their own lives.

## Key Terms

**theocracy**  a government that is ruled by religious leaders

**totalitarianism**  authoritarian rule that controls nearly every aspect of public and private
life in a country

**communism**  an economic and political system in which government owns all property
and controls economic planning

## Taking Notes

As you read the summaries, use your Student Casebook to take notes on
the section.

## Case Study Summary

### TOTALITARIAN RULE IN NORTH KOREA

After World War II, the United States and the Soviet
Union divided the country of Korea into two parts.
Occupied by the Soviet Union, North Korea
established a government partially based on Soviet
communism. Kim Il Sung became the country's
leader, a totalitarian dictator who worked to control all
aspects of life.

Today, Kim Il Jung's son, Kim Jong Il, rules North
Korea much as his father did. The country is isolated
from the rest of the world but is known for its
widespread civil and human rights abuses. Citizens'
"right to vote" is limited to voting for the one
candidate the country's ruling political party, the
Korean Workers' Party, chooses for the ballot. Many
North Koreans live in extreme poverty, and failed
government programs, natural disasters, and the
collapse of the Soviet Union have led to millions of
deaths from starvation. With serious economic
problems, North Korea accepts much-needed foreign
aid. However, its work on nuclear weapons has further
harmed its relations with other countries.

> **What is North Korea's relationship with other countries?**
> _____
> _____

# What You Need to Know Summary

## AUTHORITARIAN SYSTEMS

In an authoritarian system, all power rests with a single leader or small group—citizens have no way to influence or change government, even if there is the appearance of democratic rule. There are many forms of authoritarianism. In a **theocracy**, a government is ruled by religious leaders, who believe that government authority rests with God or some divine power, not the people. In a dictatorship, the most common form of authoritarian rule, dictators may take power by overthrowing the previous government or even by first being elected. **Totalitarianism** occurs when authoritarian rule controls nearly every aspect of public and private life in a country. The government controls everything, and citizens have no freedom of choice.

Authoritarian systems, though they can vary, share some common features. Citizens' civil and human rights are rarely or never protected and rulers may use force to squelch opposition. Also, authoritarian governments are not limited by existing law—rulers can change or ignore any restrictions on their power.

> **What do authoritarian systems have in common?**
> _____
> _____
> _____

## THE SOVIET UNION AND CHINA

In 1922 revolutionaries led by Vladimir Lenin formed the Soviet Union around the theory of **communism**, an economic and political system in which government owns all property and controls economic planning. The Soviet government severely limited citizens' rights and allowed only one political party, the Communist Party of the Soviet Union (CPSU), which was controlled by the Central Committee. This committee elected the Politburo, the chief decision-making body. The Politburo was headed by a general secretary who was also the Soviet leader. In 1928 Joseph Stalin took control of the country, instituting a totalitarian regime under which millions of citizens were killed and imprisoned. After Stalin's death in 1953, restrictions on Soviet citizens were eased a bit, but it was not until reforms took place in the 1980s that Soviet power truly began to weaken.

The People's Republic of China was established in 1949, led by Mao Zedong, who imprisoned or killed

> **Describe the structure of the Soviet Union's government.**
> _____
> _____
> _____

those who spoke out against his policies—including a failed five-year Soviet-style plan for economic development that led to deadly food shortages. After Zedong's death in 1976, some economic and political reforms were put into place by leader Deng Xiaoping. Today while some changes have been made, the communist government still limits citizens' basic rights and freedoms. The Chinese Communist Party (CCP) rules the country, electing a Central Committee, which elects the Politburo—a small decision-making body led by a general secretary who is often also China's president. The State Council is the country's chief executive body, led by a premier chosen by the president. The National People's Congress consists of elected representatives, who mainly carry out State Council and CCP decisions.

> **Does the National People's Congress carry out its constituents' wishes? Explain.**
>
> _____
>
> _____

## OTHER AUTHORITARIAN NATIONS

Although it is now a democracy, Chile was under authoritarian rule for years, most recently under General Augusto Pinochet, a military leader who overthrew the socialist government in 1973. For years, Pinochet's government committed human rights abuses, and thousands were tortured and killed. In 1988 Pinochet allowed Chileans to vote as to whether he should stay in power. He was quickly voted out in favor of open elections.

Italy and Germany, also both modern democracies, first underwent periods of fascism—the glorification of the state above all else, including individual needs—in the years between World Wars I and II. Italian dictator Benito Mussolini and German fascist leader Adolf Hitler—under whom millions of Jews were killed—were both defeated during World War II.

Saudi Arabia, an oil-rich U.S. ally, remains an authoritarian nation. Its monarch has near-absolute power but must also follow the Qur'an, the sacred text of Islam, and the laws of Islam. The government tightly controls its people and spends much of its money on social programs and the military. National elections and political parties do not exist.

> **Who led the fascist governments of Italy and Germany?**
>
> _____
>
> _____
>
> _____

# Simulation

Use your Student Casebook to help you complete the simulation.

## Comparative Political and Economic Systems

**READING FOCUS**
Economic systems can be characterized as three basic types: traditional, market, and command. Nearly all nations today have mixed economies, meaning they have some combination of traditional, market, and command features.

# Key Terms

**factors of production** the basic resources that make up an economy—land and natural resources, labor, and capital

**traditional economy** an economy in which people answer the basic economic questions by custom

**market economy** an economy in which individuals and businesses make most economic decisions

**command economy** an economy in which the government makes most economic decisions

**mixed economy** an economy that combines elements of traditional, market, and command economies

**capitalism** a type of mixed economy in which individuals and businesses make most economic decisions

**laissez-faire** a concept popularized by Adam Smith that calls for minimal government involvement in economic affairs

**socialism** an economic and political system in which the state controls most productive resources

**proletariat** working class

**bourgeoisie** the people who own the means of production in a capitalist system

# Taking Notes

As you read the summaries, use your Student Casebook to take notes on the section.

# Case Study Summary

## A CHANGING INDIA

Once India won its independence from Great Britain in 1947, leaders established socialist policies in hopes of encouraging economic growth by spreading wealth equally among the population. The government took control of and regulated all key industries, a move that resulted in economic slowdown starting in the 1960s.

By the 1970s, India began making the transition to an economy based on free markets, leaving more

economic decisions to individuals and businesses. The
Indian economy accelerated in the 1990s, and once the
government lowered barriers to foreign trade, there
was a dramatic increase in competition, efficiency,
and foreign investment. Today India's economy is still
booming and a widespread middle class has
developed. However, the country still faces many
challenges, including how to help the 30 percent of
the population living in poverty and how to
adequately expand the national infrastructure.

> **What change did India's government make to turn around its economy?**
>
> _____
>
> _____

## MAKING ECONOMIC DECISIONS

Economics is the study of how people produce,
distribute, and consume goods and services. The basic
resources that make up an economy—land and natural
resources, labor, and capital—are known as the
**factors of production**. All societies consider the
questions of what should be produced, how, and for
whom when deciding how to use resources to provide
goods and services. In a **traditional economy**, people
answer these questions by custom, or what has always
been done. In a **market economy**, individuals and
business make most economic decisions based on the
needs and wants of others. Finally, in a **command
economy**, the government makes most economic
decisions. Today most countries have a **mixed
economy**, which combines elements of all additional,
market, and command economies.

## MIXED ECONOMIES

There are three main types of mixed economies:
capitalism, socialism, and communism. The U.S.
economy is largely based on **capitalism**, in which
individuals and businesses make most economic
decisions and competition is encouraged. Philosopher
Adam Smith founded capitalism, encouraging **laissez-
faire** practices, or minimal government involvement
in economic affairs. While government still plays an
important role in all capitalist economies—such as by
encouraging job creation—the United States and
many other governments are working toward reduced
government involvement in international trade and
encouraging global competition.

> **What role do individuals play in a capitalist economy?**
>
> _____
>
> _____

The second type of mixed economy is **socialism**, an economic and political system in which the state controls most productive resources, mainly in order to distribute wealth throughout society for the benefit of the majority of its citizens. German theorist Karl Marx founded modern socialism, arguing that in a capitalist society, the **proletariat**, or working class, receives unfair treatment from the **bourgeoisie**, or the people who own the means of production. Today most socialist countries are democratic, resolving any injustices of capitalism with regulation and plentiful social services, such as retirement benefits and child care. Opponents of socialism argue that all of these social programs lead to high taxes, and that since everyone has to pay these taxes, there is little incentive to work harder or more creatively. Supporters counter that capitalism produces inequalities, an ill fixed by the economic democracy of socialism.

Karl Marx believed that the proletariat would overthrow capitalism, resulting in a classless society he called *Communist*. Today communism is the third type of mixed economy, first adopted by the leaders of the Soviet Union. There the government owned most businesses and resources and controlled all economic planning. This system resulted in increased industrialization and a powerful military but also created inefficiencies and high costs. The Soviet empire collapsed in 1991.

However, Communist China, established in 1949, still exists, having gradually moved away from central planning and communism toward increased economic freedoms for businesses and foreign investment. China is now projected to be the second largest economy in the world.

While communism is basically an extreme authoritarian form of socialism, it can allow countries to develop their economies quickly. Yet in an economy that does not allow competition, poor product quality and shortages of consumer goods can become worrisome problems.

> **What are the arguments for and against socialism?**
> _____
> _____
> _____

> **How might a lack of competition hurt an economy?**
> _____
> _____
> _____

## Simulation

Use your Student Casebook to help you complete the simulation.

Name _____ Class _____ Date _____

## State and Local Government

# Chapter Summary

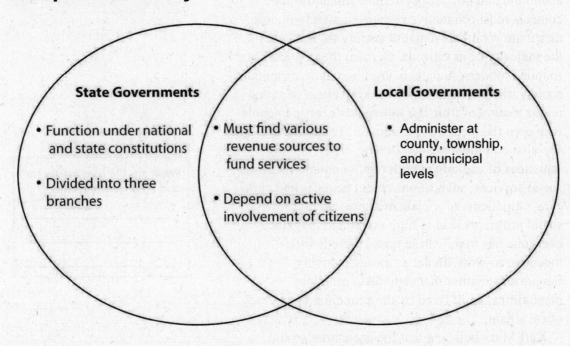

**State Governments**

- Function under national and state constitutions

- Divided into three branches

**Must find various revenue sources to fund services**

**Depend on active involvement of citizens**

**Local Governments**

- Administer at county, township, and municipal levels

## COMPREHENSION AND CRITICAL THINKING

Use information from the graphic organizer to answer the following questions.

1. **Recall** How is power divided in state governments?

_____

_____

2. **Analyze** Local governments must provide many services. How do you think active citizen participation affects the delivery of these services?

_____

_____

3. **Evaluate** Why do you think the structure of state government is so similar to that of the federal government?

_____

_____

_____

**State and Local Government**

> **READING FOCUS**
> As you have learned, the word *federalism* is used to describe the relationship between the national and state governments. State governments function under the national constitution and a state constitution. State constitutions share important similarities as well as strengths and weaknesses.

## Key Terms

**guarantee clause** another name for Article IV, Section 4, of the Constitution, which "guarantee[s] to every state in [the] Union a Republic Form of Government"

**fundamental law** law that determines the basic political principles of a government

**statutory law** law found in state constitutions that is very detailed and specific

## Taking Notes

As you read the summaries, use your Student Casebook to take notes on the section.

## Case Study Summary

### THE NULLIFICATION CRISIS

In 1828 Congress raised a tariff on British imports to help goods produced in the northern states seem less expensive. The southern states quickly protested what they called the Tariff of Abominations, claiming that the tariff hurt them in favor of the northern states. Even after a new, lower tariff was passed, the South Carolina legislature remained furious and voted to test the doctrine of nullification, only a theory up until that point. By passing the Ordinance of Nullification in November 1832, the state nullified, or disregarded, the federal tariff, judging them to be against the state's best interests.

President Andrew Jackson issued the Nullification Proclamation the next month, declaring South Carolina's ordinance illegal. Tensions between South Carolina and the federal government remained strained until the Compromise Tariff of 1833, which gradually reduced tariff rates, went into effect. Yet states' rights remained a national issue, eventually becoming one of the causes of the Civil War. While the Supreme Court ruled in *Texas* v. *White* (1869) that the United States was "an indestructible Union, composed of indestructible states," states' rights are

> Why did South Carolina's legislature nullify the 1828 tariff?
> _____
> _____
> _____

still the focus of many political debates today,
including those surrounding civil rights and gun laws.

# What You Need to Know Summary

## STATES IN THE FEDERAL SYSTEM

Although the Constitution grants delegated powers to
the national government and reserves all other powers
to the states—besides those powers held concurrently
by both levels of government—it was inevitable that
conflicts would arise between the national and state
governments. The Framers anticipated this and
included the supremacy clause in Article 6, Section 2,
of the Constitution, which declares the laws of the
national government the "supreme law of the land."
The Framers also anticipated the need for guidelines
for relationships between states, exemplified by their
inclusion of the full faith and credit clause. This
clause requires that each state recognize the civil laws
and acts, as well as the decisions of the courts, of the
other states. The full faith and credit clause was
intended to promote and ease cooperation between the
states.

> **What does the inclusion of the supremacy clause in the Constitution show about the Framers?**
> _____
> _____

## STATE CONSTITUTIONS

Article IV, Section 4, of the Constitution, also known
as the **guarantee clause**, "guarantees to every state in
[the] Union a Republican Form of Government."
Through this clause, the Constitution ensures that state
governments will be limited and representative like
the national government, but leaves all other decisions
about the framework of state and local governments to
each state's constitution.

State constitutions vary in length and how many
times they have been rewritten, but all express basic
civic principles and practices and include a bill of
rights. While the government outlined by each state
constitution is different from those of other states,
every state government is limited, with power shared
between its legislative, executive, and judicial
branches.

> **What do state constitutions have in common?**
> _____
> _____

The state constitutions have been amended many
more times than the U.S. Constitution, primarily
because the process for making changes is easier.
Most state constitutions have also been rewritten more

than once, although some states still have original constitutions, including Massachusetts, which has the world's oldest constitution still in effect.

The number of rewrites most state constitutions have undergone over the centuries has resulted in some problems. Many constitutions are extremely long, due to the fact that they contain both **fundamental law**—law determining the fundamental political principles of a government, as in the U.S. Constitution—and **statutory law**—detailed, specific, and often obsolete law. To address the problem of excessive statutory law, several states have revised or completely rewritten their constitutions, sometimes through the amendment process.

> **Why is statutory law sometimes a problem in state constitutions?**
> _____
> _____

## Simulation

Use your Student Casebook to help you complete the simulation.

## State and Local Government

**READING FOCUS**
State governments, like the federal government, divide power among legislative, executive, and judicial branches. In terms of their structure and functions, these state branches mirror the branches of the federal government. Also like the federal government, state governments must find funding for expensive yet essential programs and services.

# Key Terms

**governor** the chief executive in a state government

**citizen legislatures** part-time legislatures, in which legislators meet only once every other year and for a period of about two months

**professional legislatures** legislature in which sessions may be held annually and may last for much of the year

**line-item veto** a type of veto by which a governor can reject specific parts of legislation while signing the rest of a bill into law

**executive clemency** powers granted to a governor, including the power to grant pardons and commutations

**Missouri Plan** a system for selecting judges involving both election and appointment

# Taking Notes

As you read the summaries, use your Student Casebook to take notes on the section.

# Case Study Summary

## TEEN DRIVING LAWS

In July 2003, 17-year-old Joshua Brown from Georgia lost control of his car on a wet road and died upon colliding with a tree. In response to this tragedy, the state legislature passed Joshua's Law, legislation that expanded Georgia's already strict licensing system for teen drivers. Sixteen-year-olds now have to take driver education classes to apply for unrestricted licenses and all teen drivers must undergo hours of supervised driving.

As the history of Joshua's Law shows, driving laws are the responsibility of the state—and these laws vary widely. In some states, teens can drive without supervision at 14 and a half, while the beginner's age is 16 and a half in other states. Most states have

> How did Joshua's Law change Georgia's licensing system for teen drivers?
>
> _____
>
> _____

graduated licensing systems, which usually involve a learner's permit and periods of restricted driving.

# What You Need to Know Summary

## ORGANIZATION OF STATE GOVERNMENTS

As in the federal government, power is divided between three branches in state government. State legislatures are bicameral, except in Nebraska, where the legislature is unicameral. The lower house is usually called the House of Representatives and the upper house the Senate. Total number of legislators, terms of office, and session lengths vary, but state legislatures share some common features. State executive branches are also similar. All 50 states have an elected **governor**, who serves as chief executive of state. The state judicial branch is the third arm of state government and includes both trial and appellate courts. State courts hear cases involving state law, which make up 99 percent of all U.S. court cases.

> **Name three ways in which the structure of state governments is similar to that of the federal government.**
>
> _____
>
> _____
>
> _____

## STATE LEGISLATIVE BRANCHES

State legislatures can be citizen legislatures, professional legislatures, or a combination of both. There are 17 **citizen legislatures,** in which legislators meet only once every other year and for a period of about two months. There are 11 **professional legislatures**, in which sessions may be held annually and last for much of the year. Legislators in this type of legislature do not usually hold other jobs, as do those in citizen legislatures.

A state legislature is granted all of the reserved powers not granted to another branch by the state constitution and not denied it by the state constitution or the U.S. Constitution. The power to make laws is key to state legislatures, whose actions often influence the U.S. Congress. Also, the legislatures' approval and impeachment powers allow them to check the other state branches. The organization and law-making processes of state legislatures resemble those of U.S. Congress, including the roles of presiding officers and committees and how a bill becomes law.

> **What is the difference between citizen and professional legislatures?**
>
> _____
>
> _____
>
> _____

## STATE EXECUTIVE BRANCHES

Governors have many powers, including the power to enforce state law and mobilize the state's units of the National Guard. The governor can check the other branches by vetoing legislation—in most states, a **line-item veto** allows the governor to reject only specific parts of legislation—and using the powers of **executive clemency**. Most governors serve four-year terms. Governors work closely with other key executive officers, which can include the lieutenant governor, secretary of state, state treasurers, and attorney general.

> **What is the purpose of a line-item veto?**
> _____
> _____

## STATE JUDICIAL BRANCHES

State courts hear both civil and criminal cases. In criminal cases, a grand jury decides if there is enough evidence to indict a person. A petit jury then hears the case. If a person is found guilty, he or she may appeal the decision to the state's intermediate appellate court and sometimes then to the state supreme court. From there, a very few cases involving federal law or the Constitution can move to the federal court system.

State judges are either appointed by the governor or legislature, elected, or both appointed and elected under a form of the **Missouri Plan**. Under this plan, the governor appoints a judge based on a list compiled by a nonpartisan commission. At the next election, voters can then choose to keep or replace the judge.

> **Explain the Missouri Plan in your own words.**
> _____
> _____
> _____
> _____

## STATE SERVICES AND FINANCES

States must provide many essential government services, ranging from funding and shaping education to maintaining roads. To fund services, most states collect income and sales taxes, as well as charge user fees, receive federal grants, sell bonds, and run a lottery. The state budget—which must be balanced in many states—is developed by the governor, revised by the legislature, and approved by the governor.

# Simulation

Use your Student Casebook to help you complete the simulation.

## State and Local Government

**READING FOCUS**
A variety of local governments provide many of the services you rely on every day. These services are paid for by local, state, and federal revenue. Direct citizen participation in government is often easiest at the local level.

# Key Terms

**counties** the most basic units of government, except for in parts of New England

**parishes** counties in Louisiana

**boroughs** counties in Alaska

**townships** divisions of counties

**municipalities** the nation's cities, towns, and villages

**incorporation** process by which municipalities are given their legal authority by the state

**mayor-council system** a form of municipal government in which citizens elect a mayor to serve as the chief executive and a city council to serve as the local legislature

**council-manager system** a form of municipal government in which the city council appoints a city manager to be the chief executive and the mayor leads the city council

**commission system** a form of municipal government in which a group of elected commissioners lead city departments and set local policies

**special districts** local governments that provide a single service to defined area

**zoning laws** laws passed by cities and towns to regulate land use

**initiative** a process through which citizens propose and enact state and local laws directly

**referendum** a popular vote on a proposal that has already been considered by the legislature

**recall** a process through which citizens remove government officials from office before the end of a term

# Taking Notes

As you read the summaries, use your Student Casebook to take notes on the section.

# Case Study Summary

### LAND USE IN EASTON, MARYLAND

In the United States, local governments regularly make decisions about how land should be used and how to balance economic growth with potential community concerns. In 1999 the town of Easton, Maryland, was faced with the dilemma of whether it should allow three "big-box" retail stores to locate to their 14,000-person town. Residents raised many concerns, such as whether local roads could handle the increased traffic the stores would attract and how the large stores would affect the town's smaller retailers and overall charm.

In order to address these concerns, the town government issued a moratorium on the construction of big-box stores, then held hearings and commissioned a study on the effects of large-scale development on Easton. When the local government determined that stores larger than 65,000 feet would indeed harm the town, the Easton Planning and Zoning Commissions recommended prohibiting the building of stores that size. In response, the Easton Town Council issued an ordinance that made this recommendation into law.

> **What steps did the Easton town government take to address residents' concerns?**
> _____
> _____
> _____

# What You Need to Know Summary
## LOCAL GOVERNMENT

There are approximately 88,000 local governments in the United States, each created by its home state. There are various levels of local government. All states are divided into **counties**, which are the most basic units of government except in parts of New England; counties are called **parishes** in Louisiana and **boroughs** in Alaska. Most counties are governed by county boards. In certain parts of the country where counties are divided into **townships**, township governments help the county government deliver services, especially to rural areas.

In addition to counties and townships, Americans also live in **municipalities**—the nation's nearly 20,000 cities, towns, and villages, each given legal authority by the state through a process called **incorporation**. There are three forms of municipal government. First, in the **mayor-council system**, citizens elect a mayor to serve as the chief executive and a city council to serve as the local legislature. Second, in the **council-manager system**, the city council appoints a city manager to be the chief executive and the mayor leads the city council. Finally, in a **commission system**, a group of elected commissioners lead city departments and set local

> **Which level of government do you think would best be able to meet citizens' specific needs: county or municipal government? Explain.**
> _____
> _____
> _____
> _____

policies. In certain parts of New England where towns, not counties, are the most basic units of government, a board of three to five selectmen presides over town meetings and manages the town's affairs. The greatest number of local governments are **special districts**, which provide a single service to a defined area, such as school districts.

County governments provide many essential services, such as public safety, record keeping, and election supervision. Municipal governments provide additional services, including libraries and garbage collection. Municipal governments also regulate land use in the area through **zoning laws**.

Local governments need to raise money to cover the costs of these services. They do this mainly by collecting property taxes on much of the land, homes, cars, and business property within their boundaries. A local government may also levy additional sales and income taxes, tax corporations, charge certain user fees, or sell municipal bonds. Intergovernmental revenue, such as federal and state grants, can also help local governments fund services.

> **What is the purpose of zoning laws?**
> _____
> _____

## PARTICIPATING IN STATE AND LOCAL GOVERNMENT

When citizens monitor public policy and make their interests known to government officials, they are taking part in a process called participatory citizenship. Voting, running for office, volunteering, and testifying before state or local boards are all ways to be an active citizen. Some citizen actions actually have the force of law, such as an **initiative**, a process through which citizens propose and enact state and local laws directly. In an initiative, citizens collect signatures on a petition supporting a bill, then either pass it to the state legislature or the state's voters for approval. Citizens can also make laws through a **referendum**, a popular vote on a proposal that has already been considered by the legislature, and remove government officials from office before the end of a term through a **recall**.

> **What can citizens accomplish through an initiative?**
> _____
> _____

## Simulation

Use your Student Casebook to help you complete the simulation.